IMAGE EVALUATION
TEST TARGET (MT-3)

6"

Photographic
Sciences
Corporation

33 WEST MAIN STREET
WEBSTER, N.Y. 14580
(716) 872-4503

CIHM/ICMH
Microfiche
Series.

CIHM/ICMH
Collection de
microfiches.

Canadian Institute for Historical Microreproductions / Institut canadien de microreproductions historiques

© 1982

Technical and Bibliographic Notes/Notes techniques et bibliographiques

The Institute has attempted to obtain the best original copy available for filming. Features of this copy which may be bibliographically unique, which may alter any of the images in the reproduction, or which may significantly change the usual method of filming, are checked below.

L'Institut a microfilmé le meilleur exemplaire qu'il lui a été possible de se procurer. Les détails de cet exemplaire qui sont peut-être uniques du point de vue bibliographique, qui peuvent modifier une image reproduite, ou qui peuvent exiger une modification dans la méthode normale de filmage sont indiqués ci-dessous.

- [X] Coloured covers/
  Couverture de couleur
- [X] Covers damaged/
  Couverture endommagée
- [ ] Covers restored and/or laminated/
  Couverture restaurée et/ou pelliculée
- [ ] Cover title missing/
  Le titre de couverture manque
- [ ] Coloured maps/
  Cartes géographiques en couleur
- [ ] Coloured ink (i.e. other than blue or black)/
  Encre de couleur (i.e. autre que bleue ou noire)
- [ ] Coloured plates and/or illustrations/
  Planches et/ou illustrations en couleur
- [ ] Bound with other material/
  Relié avec d'autres documents
- [ ] Tight binding may cause shadows or distortion along interior margin/
  La reliure serrée peut causer de l'ombre ou de la distortion le long de la marge intérieure
- [ ] Blank leaves added during restoration may appear within the text. Whenever possible, these have been omitted from filming/
  Il se peut que certaines pages blanches ajoutées lors d'une restauration apparaissent dans le texte, mais, lorsque cela était possible, ces pages n'ont pas été filmées.
- [ ] Additional comments:/
  Commentaires supplémentaires:

- [ ] Coloured pages/
  Pages de couleur
- [ ] Pages damaged/
  Pages endommagées
- [ ] Pages restored and/or laminated/
  Pages restaurées et/ou pelliculées
- [X] Pages discoloured, stained or foxed/
  Pages décolorées, tachetées ou piquées
- [ ] Pages detached/
  Pages détachées
- [X] Showthrough/
  Transparence
- [ ] Quality of print varies/
  Qualité inégale de l'impression
- [ ] Includes supplementary material/
  Comprend du matériel supplémentaire
- [ ] Only edition available/
  Seule édition disponible
- [ ] Pages wholly or partially obscured by errata slips, tissues, etc., have been refilmed to ensure the best possible image/
  Les pages totalement ou partiellement obscurcies par un feuillet d'errata, une pelure, etc., ont été filmées à nouveau de façon à obtenir la meilleure image possible.

This item is filmed at the reduction ratio checked below/
Ce document est filmé au taux de réduction indiqué ci-dessous.

10X	14X	18X	22X	26X	30X
		✓			
12X	16X	20X	24X	28X	32X

WESLEYAN
CONFERENCE MEMORIAL
ON THE QUESTION OF
LIBERAL EDUCATION
IN
UPPER CANADA,
EXPLAINED AND DEFENDED
BY
Numerous Proofs and Illustrations,
BY A COMMITTEE.

REPRINTED FROM THE "CHRISTIAN GUARDIAN"

Toronto:
PRINTED AT THE GUARDIAN STEAM PRESS.
1860.

WESLEYAN

CONFERENCE MEMORIAL

ON THE QUESTION OF

LIBERAL EDUCATION

IN

UPPER CANADA,

EXPLAINED AND DEFENDED

BY

Numerous Proofs and Illustrations,

BY A COMMITTEE.

REPRINTED FROM THE "CHRISTIAN GUARDIAN."

Toronto:
PRINTED AT THE GUARDIAN STEAM PRESS.
1860.

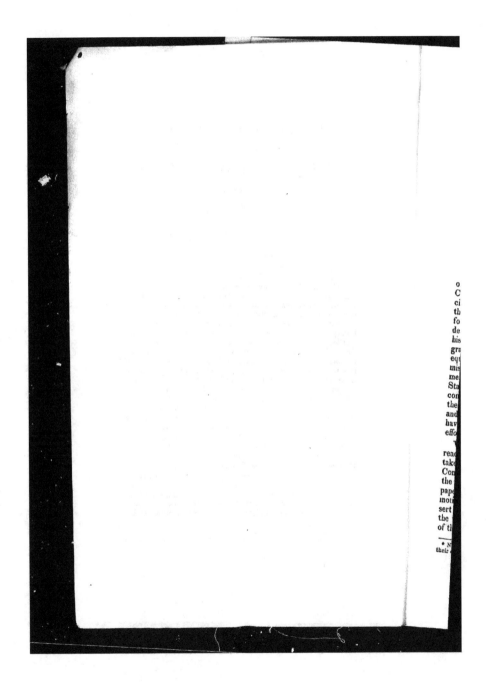

APPEAL OF THE WESLEYAN CONFERENCE

IN FAVOUR OF THE DIFFUSION OF

LIBERAL EDUCATION

THROUGHOUT

UPPER CANADA.

(Reprinted from the Christian Guardian.)

INTRODUCTION.

We publish this day, (Nov. 30, 1859) the Memorial prepared by order and in behalf of the Conference of the Wesleyan Methodist Church in Canada to the Legislature, on the questions of the Provincial University, and Colleges for Upper Canada. We commend this document as an exposition of the views and feelings of more than four hundred Christian Ministers;—a body of men whose self-denying labours stretch back to the earliest period of Canadian history, and extend to the remotest townships of Canadian immigration: a body of men who have been the pioneer champions of equal religious liberty in Canada, as they have been the pioneer missionaries to its new settlements and Indian tribes; a body of men who have repeatedly refused to receive anything from the State which was not equally available to every other religious community; who have never asked anything for themselves or their own community except upon the principles of equal justice and rights to all religious denominations and classes, and who have made the first and most persevering exertions by voluntary efforts to promote academical education in the country.

We recommend this memorial to the attentive perusal of every reader, and especially of those editors and writers who have mistaken and misrepresented the views and objects of the Wesleyan Conference in regard to the Provincial University. We trust the *Globe*, and *Leader*, and *Montreal Witness*,* and other newspapers in which erroneous interpretations of the sentiments and motives of the Wesleyan Conference have been admitted, will insert this exposition of the views and requests of that body upon the whole question of the higher as well as elementary education of the country.

---

* Neither the Toronto *Globe* nor *Montreal Witness* has inserted the Memorial in their columns.

4

' We appeal to statesmen of all parties, to the clergy and members of all religious persuasions, to ponder and compare the liberal, just, and philanthropic views of this appeal of the Wesleyan Conference with the exclusive, selfish, and petty effusions of their assailants. We appeal to every philanthropist, to every thinking man of every party, whether the remonstrances and recommendations of the Wesleyan Conference do not, in an economical, Christian, and national point of view, redound infinitely more to the highest and best educational interests of Upper Canada than the wasteful and contracted proceedings of the Toronto monopolists. The Wesleyan Conference has taken its stand upon the plain intentions of the Legislature, as well as of justice and patriotism, while the proceedings of the Senate of the University have been in plain violation of those intentions.

The only practical argument employed by these champions of extravagance and monopoly, is the senseless bug-bear of "sectarian education," as if it were not better for men to be educated with decided religious principles and feelings than with no religious principles and feelings; as if the religious principles of a university education at Oxford, Cambridge and Dublin, were an evil to be dreaded, and every graduate of either of those seats of learning was a monster to be avoided until he abandoned the faith of his education; as if that to which Scotland owes its highest glory, were a calamity to be deprecated, and as if every Scotch Minister in Canada who had graduated at a Scotch University, were a living beacon of warning against the evils of "sectarian education," as if they would have been so much better men had Christianity, and decided denominational Christianity too, never been blended with their university education. There may be degenerate men from Oxford, Cambridge and Dublin, who now profess to deprecate what they gloried in until a college monopoly was usurped by them. There may be Scotch graduates who, because a college monopoly can be turned to their account, will now exclaim against that of which they have ever before justly boasted as Scotchman, and ministers and scholars; but every sound hearted man among them all, may be appealed to, whether he regards the religious influences of his university education as an evil, and not a benefit, and whether he does not believe it would have been better rather than worse for him had those religious influences been more powerful and more practical than they were. We appeal to the consciousness and conscience of the Presbyterian minister and scholar against the pretension of the Toronto Monopolists; and we appeal to the same consciousness and conscience of the graduate of Oxford, Cambridge, or Dublin against the same pretensions.

We ask for no Sectarian University; nay we desire a non-

denominational, an impartial university to confer degrees in Science Literature and Art; but we ask for equal aid for a collegiate education which will blend the daily influences of religion with the daily studies of literature and science, which developes the moral as well as the intellectual man, which trains the heart to divine virtue, while it stores the understanding with human learning.

As the embellishment of a private edifice is no proof of the intelligence and virtues of its occupants; as the marble and ornate splendour of the church edifice are no guarantee or indication of the ability and soundness of its pulpit discourse; so the costly magnificence of the collegiate edifice is no proof or security of even mediocrity in its standard, or system, or principles, or methods of instruction. History teaches that just in proportion as Greece and Rome lavished their resources upon stone and marble, upon the material and inanimate, they declined in the intellectual and moral; and we cannot but look upon the diminution of several thousand pounds a year in the available resources for promoting collegiate education in Upper Canada, by the lavishing of one hundred thousand pounds instead of expending one hundred thousand dollars, upon a collegiate edifice in Toronto, as the dictate of vanity and selfishness rather than of wisdom and patriotism, as portentous of evil rather than of good to our country. Ours is not the country, nor even the age, in which the necessary, the practical, and the useful are to be sacrificed to the " lust of the eye, and the pride of life," in which what has been set apart for other objects, and what should be husbanded and applied as a sacred treasure for the liberal education of the largest number of the rising and future generations of Canada, is wasted by thousands in mosaics and corbels, in an institution which ought not to be intended for *show* but for *work*, and in a comparatively new and poor country, where every farthing is required to aid the education of youth.

Far be it from us to object to what is convenient and appropriate, and even plainly elegant in an educational structure, whether a school or a college; but when it is considered how simple and plain are the halls and lecture rooms, in which the most learned Professors in Europe have lectured to princes and nobles as well as to plebeians, and where the profoundest intellects that ever thought have been trained, we cannot but grieve that such examples are not followed in Upper Canada, and that the most precious and largest of our educational funds should be lavished upon what may make the City of Toronto proud instead of making the youth of Upper Canada learned.

TO THE LEGISLATIVE COUNCIL AND LEGISLATIVE ASSEMBLY OF CANADA:

The Memorial prepared by order and in behalf of the Conference of the Wesleyan Methodist Church in Canada,*

RESPECTFULLY SHEWETH:—

That the Legislature in passing the Provincial University Act of 1853, clearly proposed and avowed a threefold object. *First*, the creation of a University for examining candidates, and conferring degrees in the Faculties of Arts, Law, and Medicine. *Secondly*, the establishment of an elevated curriculum of University education, conformable to that of the London University in England. *Thirdly*, the association with the Provincial University of the several colleges already established, and which might be established, in Upper Canada, with the Provincial University, the same as various colleges of different denominations in Great Britain and Ireland are affiliated to the London University,—placed as they are upon equal footing in regard to and aid from the state, and on equal footing in regard to the composition of the Senate, and the appointment of examiners.

In the promotion of these objects the Conference and members of the Wesleyan Methodist Church cordially concurred; and at the first meeting after the passing of the University act, the Senatorial Board of Victoria College adopted the programme of collegiate studies established by the Senate of the London University, and referred to in the Canadian Statute. But it soon appeared that the Senate of the Toronto University, instead of giving effect to the liberal intentions of the Legislature, determined to identify the University with one college in contradistinction, and to the exclusion of all others, to establish a monopoly of senatorial power and public revenue for one college alone; so much so, that a majority of the legal quorum of the Senate now consists of the professors of one college, one of whom is invariably one of the two examiners of their own students, candidates for degrees, honors, and scholarships. The curriculum of the University studies, instead of being elevated and conformed to that of the London University, has been revised and changed three times since 1853, and reduced by options and otherwise below what it was formerly, and below what it is in the British Universities, and below what it is in the best colleges in the United States. The effect of this narrow and anti-liberal course, is, to build up one College at the expense of all others, to reduce the standard of a University degree in both Arts and Medicine below what it was before the passing of the University Act in 1853.

---

* The several propositions in this Memorial are proved and illustrated in the papers which follow.

Instead of confining the expenditure of funds to what the law prescribed—namely, the "current expenses," and such "permanent improvements or additions to the buildings," as might be necessary for the purposes of the University and University College,—new buildings have been erected at an expenditure of some hundreds of thousands of dollars, and the current expenses of the College have been increased far beyond what they were in former times of complaint and investigations on this subject.

Your Memorialists therefore submit, that in no respect have the liberal and enlightened intentions of the Legislature, in passing the University Act been fulfilled—a splendid but unjust monopoly for the City and College of Toronto having been created, instead of a liberal and elevated system, equally fair to all the colleges of the country.

A Provincial University seould be what its name imports, and what was clearly intended by the Legislature—a body equally unconnected with, and equally impartial to every college in the country; and every college should be placed on equal footing in regard to public aid *according to its works*, irrespective of place, sect, or party. It is as unjust to propose, as it is unreasonable to expect, the affiliation of several colleges in one University except on equal terms. There have been ample funds to enable the Senate to submit to the government a comprehensive and patriotic recommendation to give effect to the liberal intentions of the Legislature in the accomplishment of these objects, but the Senate has preferred to become the sole patron of one college to the exclusion of all others, and to absorb and expend the large and increasing funds of the University instead of allowing any surplus to accumulate for the general promotion of academical education, as contemplated and specifically directed by the Statute. Not only has the annual income of the University endowment been reduced some thousands of pounds per annum by vast expenditures for the erection of buildings not contemplated by the Act, but a portion of those expenditures is for the erection of lecture-rooms, &c., for the Faculties of which the Act expressly forbids the establishment!

But whilst your Memorialists complain that the very intentions of this Act have thus been disregarded and defeated, we avow our desire to be the same now as it was more than ten years ago, in favor of the establishment of a Provincial University, unconnected with any one college or religious persuasion, but sustaining a relation of equal fairness and impartiality to the several religious persuasions and colleges, with power to prescribe the curriculum to examine candidates, and confer degrees, in the Faculties of Arts, Law and Medicine.

We also desire that the University College at Toronto should be

efficiently maintained; and for that purpose we should not object that the minimum of its income from the University Endowment should be even twice that of any other college; but it is incompatible with the very idea of a national University intended to embrace the several colleges of the nation, to lavish all the endowment and patronage of the state upon one college to the exclusion of all others. At the present time, and for years past, the noble University Endowment is virtually expended by parties directly or indirectly connected with but one college, and the scholarships and prizes, the honours and degrees conferred, are virtually the rewards and praises bestowed by Professors upon their own students, and not the doings and decisions of a body wholly unconnected with the College. Degrees and distinctions thus conferred, however much they cost the country, cannot possess any higher literary value, as they are of no more legal value, than those conferred by the *Senatus Academicus* of the other chartered colleges.

It is therefore submitted that if it is desired to have one Provincial University, the corresponding arrangement should be made to place each of the colleges on equal footing according to their works in regard to everything emanating from the State. And if it is refused to place these colleges on equal footing as colleges of one University, it is but just and reasonable that they should be placed upon equal footing in regard to aid from the State according to their works as separate University colleges.

It is well known that it is the natural tendency, as all experience shows, that any college independent of all inspection, control, or competition in wealth,—all its officers securely paid by the State, independent of exertion or success,—will in a short time, as a general rule, degenerate into inactivity, indifference, and extravagence. In collegiate institutions, as well as in the higher and elementary schools, and in other public and private affairs of life, competition is an important element of efficiency and success. The best system of collegiate, as of elementary education, is that in which voluntary effort is developed by means of public aid. It is clearly both the interest and duty of the State to prompt and encourage individual effort in regard to collegiate, as in regard to elementary education, and not to discourage it by the creation of a monopoly invidious and unjust on the one side, and on the other deadening to all individual effort and enterprise, and oppressive to the State.

We submit, therefore, that justice and the best interests of liberal education require the several colleges of the country to be placed upon equal footing according to their works. We ask nothing for Victoria College which we do not ask for every Collegiate institution in Upper Canada upon the same terms.

We desire also that it may be distinctly understood that we ask

no aid towards the support of any theological school or theological chair in Victoria College. There is no such Chair in Victoria College; and whenever one shall be established, provision will be made for its support independent of any grant from the State. We claim support for Victoria College according to its works as a literary institution—as teaching those branches which are embraced in the curriculum of a liberal education, irrespective of denominational theology.

We also disclaim any sympathy with the motives and objects which have been attributed by the advocates of Toronto College monopoly, in relation to our National School system. The fact that a member of our own body has been permitted by the annual approbation of the Conference to devote himself to the establishment and extension of our school system, is ample proof of our approval of that system: in addition to which we have from time to time expressed our cordial support of it by formal resolutions, and by the testimony and example of our more than four hundred ministers throughout the Province. No religious community in Upper Canada has, therefore, given so direct and effective support to the National School system as the Wesleyan community. But we have ever maintained, and we submit, that the same interests of general education for all classes which require the maintenance of of the elementary school system require a reform in our University system in order to place it upon a foundation equally comprehensive and impartial, and not to be the patron and mouthpiece of one college alone; and the same considerations of fitness, economy, and patriotism which justify the State in co-operating with each school municipality to support a day school, require it to co-operate with each religious persuasion, according to its own educational works, to support a college. The experience of all Protestant countries shows that it is, and has been, as much the the province of a religious persuasion to establish a college, as it is for a school municipality to establish a day school; and the same experience shows that, while pastoral and parental care can be exercised for the religious instruction of children residing at home and attending a day school, that care cannot be exercised over youth residing away from home and pursuing their higher education except in a college where the pastoral and parental care can be daily combined. We hold that the highest interests of the country, as of an individual, are its religious and moral interests; and we believe there can be no heavier blow dealt out against those religious and moral interests, than for the youth of a country destined to receive the best literary education, to be placed, during the most eventful years of that educational course, without the pale of daily parental and pastoral instruction and oversight. The results of such a system must, sooner or later, sap the religious

and moral foundations of society. For such is the tendency of our nature, that with all the appliances of religious instruction and ceaseless care by the parent and pastor, they are not always successful in counteracting evil propensities and temptations; and therefore from a system which involves the withdrawal or absence of all such influences for years at a period when youthful passions are strongest and youthful temptations most powerful, we cannot but entertain painful apprehensions. Many a parent would deem it his duty to leave his son without the advantages of a liberal education, rather than thus expose him to the danger of moral shipwreck in its acquirement.

This danger does not so much apply to that very considerable class of persons whose home is in Toronto; or to those grown up young men whose character and principles are formed, and who, for the most part, are pursuing their studies by means acquired by their own industry and economy; or to the students of theological institutions established in Toronto, and to which the University College answers the convenient purpose of a free Grammar School, in certain secular branches. But such cases form the exceptions, and not the general rule. And if one college at Toronto is liberally endowed for certain classes who have themselves contributed or done nothing to promote liberal education, we submit that in all fairness, apart from moral patriotic considerations, the State ought to aid with corresponding liberality those other classes who for years have contributed largely to erect and sustain collegiate institutions, and who, while they endeavour to confer upon youth as widely as possible the advantages of a sound liberal education, seek to incorporate with it those moral influences, associations, and habits which give to education its highest value, which form the true basis and cement of civil institutions and national civilization, as well as of individual character and happiness.

We therefore pray your Honorable House, to cause an investigation to be instituted into the manner in which the University Act has been administered, and the funds of the University and Upper Canada College have been expended, the immense advantage and benefits to the country of several composing colleges over the deadening and wasteful monopoly of one College; and cause an act to be passed by which all the Colleges now established, or which may be established in Upper Canada, may be placed upon equal footing in regard to public aid, either as so many co-ordinate University Colleges, or (which we think the best system), as so many Colleges of one University.

Signed by order and in behalf of the Conference of the Wesleyan Methodist Church, in Canada,

JOSEPH STINSON, D.D., *President.*
EPHRAIM B. HARPER, *Secretary.*

PROOF AND ILLUSTRATION OF THE STATEMENTS
IN THE CONFERENCE MEMORIAL, NO. 1.

The Monopolists' fallacy exposed—Difference between a University and College—Examples—Prizes and Scholarships by wholesale—Views of the Wesleyan Body on the Question of a Provincial University, including the Colleges of the country, since 1843.

We now proceed to illustrate and prove by facts the statements of the Wesleyan Conference Memorial to the Legislature on the University and College questions. But before doing so, we must correct an error and expose a fallacy which the monopolists have most sedulously employed to delude the public in order to engross property and rights which equitably belong to others.

These exclusionists have represented throughout, that one University and one College are the same thing, and that to oppose the monopoly of one College was to oppose a Provincial University! To such an extent has this groundless and absurd pretension been carried, that, at a recent Toronto College convocation, the principal speaker announced it emphatically, and, as he said, " advisedly," as a fundamental principle and fact, that the University and College were, and must be, " one Institution!" This is the very reverse, as we shall show, of what the Parliament has declared in the University Act; the reverse of the University and College system in England; and the counterpart of what the *Leader*, with his usual force, has termed the " one horse College" system of the new States of America, where the universities are as numerous as colleges, being, in each case, " one and the same Institution:"—the very system which the Legislature, by the University Act, intended to discourage, rather than establish with the aggravated evils and downright injustice of a " one horse" college monopoly.

In refutation of the pretentious fallacy that one University and one College must be the same " Institution," we simply remark, that in England there is one *London University*, but there are *thirty-six* colleges in that University,—all standing upon equal footing—some of them Church of England, others Wesleyan, Congregational, Baptist, Roman Catholic, &c., &c. In *Oxford,* there is *one University;* but there are *twenty-four colleges*—the University having no connexion with any one College more than with another—the University Professors alone receiving any part of their salaries from the State, but unconnected with any one college, and their lectures opened to the voluntary attendance of students and graduates from all the colleges; the University ap-

pointing the Examiners, and conferring the degrees, and no Professor or Tutor, as an inviolable principle, ever examining his own students or pupils. In *Cambridge*, there is also *one University*, but there are *seventeen colleges*; and the respective relations, duties, and position of the University and colleges, are substantially the same as those of Oxford.

Now, how opposite is all this to the " one horse College" system which has been inaugurated at Toronto at a vast expense to the public. Here the highest authority in the College tells us that the University and the College must be " one Institution." Here the tutorial professor has been invariably the principal, and sometimes sole examiner of his own students, and the praises, honors, prizes, and scholarships, (always at the public expense,) bestowed upon them on his recommendation, or by his mouth, is only the Toronto monopoly method of each professor blowing his own trumpet and magnifying his own works—all, of course, at the public expense. In Oxford, there is thoroughness in the examinations, scholarships, and prizes are conferred as the reward of distinguished attainments and merits, and not as a means of attracting and multiplying students by public gratuities. Dr. Jeune, one of the Oxford Examiners, said lately in a speech at Gloucester, that "The Examiners plucked high and low," and observed—"The object is not to supply an ornamental and showy education, but to impart real, substantial, solid learning." In Toronto College, we question whether the " plucking high and low" has averaged one a-year, while there are years, as we may hereafter show, in which there were nearly as many students receiving £30 a-year, each under the name of scholars, as there were self-supporting students in the Faculty of Arts in the College. What would be thought at Oxford, Cambridge, or Dublin, or of any College in Europe, if one-half the students were salaried at the public expense, or that more than half of them were prize men and scholarship incumbents? They are not such clever professors and students in the old world. It requires the precocity of the *Leader's* " one horse" " go a-head" system of Toronto and the Western States, to produce such a multitude of collegiate prodigies—to hatch so large a proportion of its goslings into swan, and that, in Toronto exclusively, at a charge upon the public of £30 a-year each.

Let it not be imagined that we suppose the talents or attainments of the students are inferior to those of other colleges, or the professors less able and learned. But when it is claimed that that College is alone worthy of state endowment, as one priesthood or church has sometimes claimed to be the only competent and authorised instructress of the people, it becomes the duty of every honest man to show the emptiness as well as selfishness of that pretension; and ere we conclude this discussion, we shall

show that other colleges are, to say the least, as efficient and thorough and as deserving of the public support as the Toronto College; that the Toronto system has been diffused and diluted, instead of being raised as intended by the Legislature, while the system in the English Universities has been improved and elevated; that as the mind during the four years of collegiate study can only master a certain number of subjects, and a certain amount of knowledge, the system which trains critically and thoroughly in a few essential subjects, disciplines and invigorates the mental powers and gives decision of character; while the system which gives a smattering of a score of a miscellaneous subjects, dissipates and enfeebles, instead of invigorating the mental powers, and is calculated to produce supercilious conceit instead of manly energy of character. But at present, we address ourselves to the principal statements of the Wesleyan Methodist Memorial.

The first statement we propose to illustrate is that which refers to the Conference having favoured the establishment of a Provincial University, instead of being opposed to it. On this subject, as well as on every other subject of Christian and educational enterprise, the Wesleyan Conference has been long in advance of its assailants. Before some of them had ever seen Canada, and long before they thought or knew anything of a Canadian University or Colleges, the Wesleyan body had acted and spoken. More than sixteen years ago, the Senatorial Board of Victoria College (whose proceedings were confirmed by the Conference,) investigated and recorded its views on this subject at great length, and in minute detail. In 1843, the late Mr. Baldwin brought forward in behalf of the Government the first Bill for the establishment of a Provincial University. On the subject of that Bill according to the records, "A special meeting of the Board of Trustees and Visitors of Victoria College held in the College, pursuant to public notice, on Tuesday and Wednesday, the 24th and 25th of October, 1843." "After prayer, the Chairman stated the object of the meeting; after which he read a copy of a Bill now before the Provincial Legislature to provide for the *separate exercise of Collegiate and University functions of the Colleges established at the City of Toronto in Upper Canada; for incorporating certain other Colleges and Collegiate Institutions of that division of the Province with the University*, and for the more efficient establishment and satisfactory management of the same. The Board proceeded to consider the Bill, and after long and careful deliberation thereon, the following resolutions were adopted."

Then follow no less than eighteen resolutions, approving of the general principles and objects of the Bill, and making explanations for the information of the Government, and offering suggestions

for the amendment of some clauses of the Bill. We extract the 1st, 10th, 11th, and 15th of these resolutions, as they apply to our present purpose. They are as follows:

"1. This Board has observed with the greatest satisfaction and thankfulness the just and generous efforts of the Government to render the benefits of an University education accessible to all classes of the inhabitants of this Province to the greatest possible extent, without reference to forms of religious faith; securing the equitable rights and privileges of all without offence to the peculiar opinions of any, and recognizing the inspired volume as the basis of the whole system."

"10. The 15th clause of the Bill gives the convocation a power over the internal affairs of the several colleges, in regard to discipline, appointments, &c., which is incompatible with their rights, interests, and free operations. *We think the power of the Convocation over the several colleges should be restricted to the general standard and character of the education imparted in said colleges*, without interfering with the appointments, duties, or salaries of their officers, or their internal discipline."

"11. Whilst the inspiration of the Scriptures is recognized in the former part of the Bill, the 64th clause disallows the requirement of any religious qualification of any *Professor, Lecturer*, &c. We are not aware that the qualification required by the amended Charter, that every Professor or Teacher should profess his belief in the inspiration of the Scriptures and the doctrine of the Trinity, has ever been objected to on the part of any considerable portion of the community; on the contrary, we believe it has given universal satisfaction, and we should regret extremely to see that Christian provision excluded from the Charter of the University."

"15. This Board begs furthermore to state for the information of the Government, that Victoria College, from the terms of the subscriptions by which its buildings have been erected, and the provisions of the charter by which it has been incorporated, must necessarily continue to be, as it has heretofore been, a literary institution, embracing the English, as well as collegiate departments of educational instruction, open to all classes of students, without any religious test."

At a meeting of the Board of Victoria College, held in May, 1853, after the passing of the present University Act, the following proceedings took place, as recorded in the Minutes:

"The Board having had under consideration the course of study in the Faculty of Arts, and having examined the course which has been adopted by the London University, and having observed how very simple it is to that which has been adopted and pursued in

Victoria College, and having considered also that that course has been recognized and recommended by the Provincial Legislature:

"*Resolved,*—That the course of education in the Faculty of Arts prescribed by the London University, be adopted as the standard of attainments for matriculation and the degree of Bachelor of Arts in Victoria College, with the addition for the latter of Mental Philosophy: the author to be selected by the Professor in that Department; but Reid is recommended."

It is thus clear that the authorities of Victoria College have long favoured the establishment of a Provincial University, and have shown every disposition to give effect to the views of the Legislature on that subject; that the recent Memorial of the Conference reiterates views which it recorded nearly twenty years ago in favor of a Provincial University, including the several collegiate institutions of Upper Canada. If that object has not been accomplished, it has not been the fault of the Wesleyan body, but has been owing to a knot of monopolists in Toronto, who have been defeating the liberal intentions of the Legislature, and misapplying the Funds of the University, as we purpose to show in our next number.

The *Colonist* will find by referring to the extracts in the preceding article that he was quite mistaken, when on Friday last (December 2,) while courteously inserting the memorial of the Wesleyan Conference, he intimated that that body had formerly expressed different views from those embodied in the Memorial on the question of a Provincial University including the several colleges of the country.

The *Leader's* column of sneers contains not one fact or argument. His cry of "spoliation" is a poor revival under new auspices of the old cry of "spoliation" raised by the former advocates of the first King's College and the Clergy Reserve monopoly. The *Leader* writer was then fierce on the side of reform, and attacked monopoly with as much violence as he now defends it. The monopolists of the Clergy Reserves and of King's College endowment claimed to be the rightful proprietors of those revenues, and charged as "spoliation" any interference with their policy. The new monopolists of Toronto College with the *Leader* raise the same cry against a Memorial and its authors which simply asks for *investigation* and its legitimate results. They have concealed from the public their enormous expenditures of the University endowment for 1858; and they now instruct the *Leader* to cry out "spoliation" at the very proposal of enquiry into their proceeding of which the former more honorable advocates of monopoly would have been advanced.

PROOF AND ILLUSTRATION OF THE MEMORIAL
NO. 2.

First complaint of the Wesleyan Conference justified—The objects of the University Act, as declared in the Preamble and 3rd Section, defeated by the past proceedings and present composition of the Senate.

Having illustrated by facts the first statement in the Memorial of the Wesleyan Conference, that that Body has favoured, and we may add long favoured, the establishment of a Provincial University, including the several collegiate institutions of the country, as contemplated by the University Act, we now proceed to justify the first complaint in the Memorial—namely, that "the Senate of the Toronto University, instead of giving effect to the liberal intentions of the Legislature, has determined to identify the University with one College, in contradistinction, and to the exclusion of all others, to establish a monopoly of senatorial power and public revenue for one college alone; so much so, that a majority of the legal quorum of the Senate now consists of the professors of one College, one of whom is invariably one of the two examiners of their own students—candidates for degrees, honors, and scholarships."

As the preamble of an Act of Parliament declares its object or objects as well as its necessity, we prove the general scope and objects of the University Act from its preamble, which is as follows:—

"Whereas the enactments hereinafter repealed have failed to effect the end proposed by the Legislature in passing them, inasmuch as no College or Educational Institution hath under them become affiliated to the University to which they relate, and many parents and others are deterred by the expense, and other causes, from sending the youth under their charge to be educated in a large city, distant, in many cases, from their homes; and whereas from these and other causes, many do and will prosecute and complete their studies in other institutions in various parts of this Province *to whom it is just and right* to afford facilities for obtaining those scholastic honors and rewards which their diligence and proficiency may deserve, and thereby to encourage them and others to persevere in the pursuit of knowledge and sound learning; and whereas experience hath proved the principles embodied in Her Majesty's Royal Charter to the University of London in England to be well adapted for the attainment of the objects aforesaid, and for removing the difficulties and objections hereinbefore referred to: Be it enacted," &c. [Then follows the repeal of the provisions of the preceding Acts referred to.]

[Left margin fragment — partial text from torn/folded edge:]

MEMORIAL

—The objects
and 3rd Sec-
composition of

the Memorial
favoured, and
rovincial Uni-
f the country,
oceed to jus-
t "the Senate
to the liberal
ntify the Uni-
the exclusion
ower and pub-
a majority of
e professors of
two examiners
ors, and schol-

ares its object
eral scope and
which is as fol-

have failed to
passing them,
on hath under
hey relate, and
nse, and other
to be educated
ir homes; and
will prosecute
various parts of
rd facilities for
their diligence
urage them and
nd sound learn
ciples embodied
y of London in
of the objects
jections herein-
follows the re-
red to.]

17

Now nothing is more clear from this preamble, than that the Legislature contemplated the following objects:—

1. The establishment of a University at Toronto upon the same principles as those of the London University in England, which is no more connected with the University College in London than with the Congregational College at Birmingham, or the Wesleyan College at Sheffield; and which now includes thirty-six colleges, but has no connexion whatever with any one of them—they all standing upon equal footing in regard to the State, and being so many competing colleges in one University, and receiving its honors, &c., according to their works.

2. A second object clearly intended by our Legislature was *decentralising* the acquisition of collegiate education, by affording facilities and rewards for its pursuit in various parts of the Province, instead of centralising it in Toronto; an object which of course could not be accomplished without colleges in different parts of the Province, and without those colleges being placed upon equal footing in regard to the state, as in the case of the London University.

Nothing could, therefore, be more fair to all parties and more national in spirit and comprehension, than the objects of the University Act, as set forth in the preamble. But every one of these objects has been contravened by the course of proceeding adopted by the Senate of the University. They determined to patronize one College alone; and one College alone is affiliated with the University, the same as before the passing of the Act. They determined that not a sixpence of the University funds should be expended to encourage collegiate education out of Toronto, and therefore they have spent all those funds in Toronto. Had the Senate of the London University determined to patronize University College in London alone, because it was a non-denominational and secular college, and by large appropriations and every kind of aid to that college, as also by professors alone as to the course of studies, and examinations, and then getting them appointed Senators, so as to constitute a majority of its legal quorum of the Senate, does any one believe its existence would have been tolerated until this day, much less that it would have thirty-six voluntarily affiliated colleges? But the majority of the Senate of the London University felt that they were appointed for all England, and not for one town; that they had no more to do with one college than with another; that they were to know no college or party in their proceedings, but equally regard all parties according to their works, and the welfare of the whole country. Such undoubtedly, the Legislature intended should be the spirit in which the University Act of Toronto should be carried out; but how

2

opposite to this, how exclusive, how local, how sectional has been the spirit in which that Act has been administered,—and how completely have the objects proposed by the Legislature been defeated!

To show how completely separate from college, or even teaching, the Legislature intended the Toronto University to be, we quote the third clause of the University Act, as follows:

"III. There shall be no professorship or other teachership in the said *University of Toronto*, but its functions shall be limited to the examining of Candidates for degrees in the several Faculties, or for Scholarships, Prizes, or certificates of honour in different branches of knowledge, and the granting of such degrees, Sholarships, Prizes, and Certificates after examination, in the manner hereinafter mentioned."

It is perfectly clear from this clause, in connection with the preamble of the Act above quoted, without quoting other clauses, that the Legislature intended the University to be a body independent of the various colleges, and impartial towards them all; and that to the University, students from all the collegiate institutions of the country might come for examination, degrees, &c. The first appointment of Senators was made in the spirit of the Act, including the head of each College and other persons fairly selected. But there were some, residents of Toronto, who made no secret of their hostility to the Act; and it was soon made void for the purposes avowed in its preamble. Senators not resident in Toronto were not allowed any travelling expenses while attending the Senate, and meetings of it were held weekly, and sometimes oftener for months. The acting Senate thus became a local body, with local feelings and interests. But even with this advantage, all the purposes of Toronto College could not be accomplished until it was managed to get three of its Professors, in addition to the President, appointed to the Senate—thus giving Toronto College four members in a body of which five are a legal quorum. Since then Toronto College has been virtually the University, and its local and enormous expenditures for its own purposes exhibit the result. While, therefore, according to the letter of the law, the University is to have no professorship or other teachership, four professors of one college have the practical management of the University and its funds, modifying the course of study, directing the examinations, conferring degrees, scholarships, &c., at pleasure. The system, therefore, is the very antipodes of that which the Legislature intended to inaugurate by the University Act.

The title of the Act itself declares its great object to be to separate the functions of the University of Toronto from those of the College at Toronto. But the whole proceeding under that, has been

to blend the two into "one institution," by identity of control and expenditure of funds, though under the distinct names of Senate and Council. And in order to make "assurance doubly sure," for the supremacy and sole endowment of Toronto College, the large additions which have been latterly made to the Senate have all been from Students of that College, with one single exception!!!

Is it likely, is it possible under such circumstances, that any other College should become connected with the University, and thus place itself at the feet of Toronto College? If the authorities of other Colleges stood aloof until they should see whether the intentions of the Legislature would be carried into effect, and whether the contemplated Toronto University would be like London University, a National Institute, devising and recommending measures for the co-operation as far as possible of all the Colleges of the country upon equal terms, and thus combine all parties and influences in wholesome competition, in the great work of superior education, advanced to a proper and noble elevation; or whether the doings under the new Act would only be a second edition of under the former Act; the sequel has proved the necessity and wisdom of their caution. But whether other Colleges affiliated forthwith or not, or whether they should ever affiliate, the provisions of the law were not the less explicit, nor were the necessity and the wisdom less obvious and important, that the University should remain distinct from University College, instead of becoming its echo and instrument. Had no College in England affiliated with the London University, it would not have been the less unconnected with the University College in London; nor the less independent and impartial in its programmes and rewards. Not so with the Toronto University, though so intended by the Canadian Legislature. Our Legislature, in passing the Act, looked at the general interests of academical education in various parts, and among all classes in Canada disposed to help themselves; the administrators of the Act in Toronto have had a heart but for one place and one party, and have directed their effects and expended the national funds accordingly. This will be more apparent when we examine in our next paper the expenditure of the University funds in connexion with the provisions of the University Act.

PROOFS AND ILLUSTRATIONS, NO. 3.

Question stated.—Clauses of the Act authorizing expenditures of University Funds quoted—"Current Expenses" and "additions and improvements" to existing buildings alone authorized—Wherein the provisions of the Act have been perverted and violated in the expenditures of moneys, and in the application of the SURPLUS Income Fund for 1856—Increased Expenses of University College since 1845 and 1853—Evils of FUSING together the management of the University and University College—Violation of an important principle of political economy and good government. Memorial for Parliamentary investigation and interference justified.

The next complaint in the Memorial of the Wesleyan Conference which we propose to justify, is expressed in the following words:—

" Instead of confining the expenditure of the funds to what the law prescribed—namely, the 'current expenses' and such 'permanent *improvements and additions* TO THE BUILDINGS' as might be necessary for the purposes of the University and University College, new buildings have been erected at an expenditure of some hundreds of thousands of dollars, and the current expenses of the College have been increased far beyond what they were in former times of complaint and investigation on this subject."

The questions suggested by this part of our inquiry are, what expenditures did the University Act authorize? what did it direct to be done with the funds not required for these authorized expenditures? what expenditures have been made by the parties controlling the funds? and what have been the increased current expenses of University College?

The first question is, What expenditures did the University Act authorize? The 53rd and 55th Sections authorized the payment of one year's salary to certain Medical Professors, the expenses of the Bursar's office and the management of the property. Respecting these there is no question. The inquiry is, what expenditure did the Act authorize in connexion with the University and University College? The Sections referring to these are the 51st, 52nd, 56th, and 57th. The 51st Section provides that out of the University Income Fund, after paying the charges of management,

"It shall be lawful for the Governor in Council to appropriate yearly, such sum as shall be required to defray the *current expenses* of said University of Toronto, including Scholarships, Rewards and Prizes authorized by the twenty-third and twenty-fourth Sections of this Act, and to defray the *current expenses* of University College, including in both cases the care, maintenance and ordinary repairs of the property assigned for the use of the said University or College ; and with power in the Governor in Council to decide what shall be deemed *ordinary repairs* as distinguished from *permanent improvements*.

The 52nd Section authorizes the Governor in Council, " in making such appropriations for the *current expenses* of said University, or of University College, or Upper Canada College and Royal Grammar School," " to direct the particular purposes to which the whole or any part of the sum appropriated shall be applied, or to place the whole or any part *such sum* [for current expenses,] at the disposal of the Senate of said University or of the Council of said College, to be applied under provisions of Statutes in that behalf," &c.

The 56th and 57th Sections of the University Act are as follows :

" LVI. The Governor in Council shall from time to time assign for the use and purposes of the said University College and of Upper Canada College and Royal Grammar School, respectively, such *portions of property* hereby vested in the Crown, as may be necessary for the convenient *accommodation and business* of said institutions respectively ; and the property so assigned for the use of each shall be deemed to be in the legal possession and under the control of the Senate and Council of such Institutions."

LVII. The Governor in Council may authorize such permanent *improvements and additions* TO THE BUILDINGS *on the said property* as may be necessary for the purposes of the said institutions respectively, and may direct the cost thereof to be paid out of the part of the Permanent Fund aforesaid hereby made applicable to the support of the institution for the purposes of which the *improvement* or *addition* is made."

Finally, the 54th Section of the Act is as follows :—

" LIV. Any surplus of the said University Income Fund remaining at the end of any year after defraying the expenses payable out of the same, shall constitute a fund to be, from time to time, appropriated by Parliament for academical education in Upper Canada."

Such are the Sections of the Act relating to the *expenditure* of the University Funds. The 46th Section of the Act having re-invested in the Crown "all the property and effects, real and personal, of what nature or kind soever," belonging to the University and Upper Canada College; the 56th Section (above quoted) authorizes the Crown to assign "such portions of the property" as may be necessary for the premises of the University, University College, and Royal Grammar School. The other Sections quoted relate to the expenditure of the funds for the support of the University and College; and every candid man, professional or non-professional, may be appealed to as to whether the plain import and intentions of the Sections do not include simply "current expenses" of the College and University, and "additions" and *improvements* to the buildings then in existence? We appeal to any honourable man, of any persuasion or party, whether any authority can be fairly extracted from these Sections for the erection of *new* buildings on any entirely *new* site, at an expense, with their appendages, of at least *four hundred thousand dollars?* And we ask whether such a proceeding can be construed as making "*additions* and *improvements* to the buildings" already erected on the University property? Is there a man in Canada, or anywhere else, that would mean by "additions and improvement" to his buildings the entire abandonment of them, and the selection of a new site and the erection of new buildings of fifty times the cost of those already erected, and which were still almost new? Yet those Sections are the sole authority for this enormous outlays of the University funds in the erection of the most magnificent and expensive buildings of the kind in America,—but so much for show, that they contain accommodations for only *sixty resident* students! Then there is not one word in the Act that authorizes or implies the founding of a Library or Museum; but *twenty thousand pounds* have already been appropriated for them! We speak not here of the wisdom of such appropriations, but of the authority for making them.

In the Sections of the Act quoted, the words "current expenses" occur again and again. No man can mistake their meaning. And the 54th Section of the Act (also quoted above) clearly intended and *required* that the income of *each year* remaining after defraying such "current expenses," and those of necessary "additions and improvements of the building," (which could only rarely occur,) should "*constitute a fund* to be appropriated by Parliament for academical education in Upper Canada." In the Printed Bill as brought into the Legislature, there were two Sections in the place of the present 54th Section of the Act. Those Sections provided for making a minimum grant to each of the other colleges in Upper Canada; clearly showing that it was

the deliberate and declared policy of the Government of 1853, with the distinguished Earl of Elgin at its head, to aid the other colleges, out of the University endowment, as well as to provide for the "current expenses" of Toronto College. But when it was apprehended that the income of that endowment was not then sufficient for those purposes, the proposed Sections were superseded by the 54th Section of the Act above quoted.

In all fairness and honesty, then, the parties having the management of the Fund should have seen that the annual expenditure of its income was economically and faithfully confined to the purposes specified in the Act, and that the surplus income was set apart and reported for appropriation by Parliament as provided by the 54th Section. But nothing of the kind has been done. Not only have unprecedented expenditures of every kind been made, but when notwithstanding, from the very great increase of the Fund, a *surplus* occurred at the end of 1856, amounting to £6922 19s 9d instead of setting it apart as *expressly required* by the 54th Section of the Act, to "constitute a Fund to be appropriated by Parliament for academical education in Upper Canada," £1500 of that surplus was loaned (virtually given) to Upper Canada College, and the balance carried to the amount of 1857; and then and there it disappears from view; but how we are left to conjecture. A convenient influence seems to have been employed to prevent the financial accounts of the University from being printed in 1858—the only public account, as far as we know, which have not been printed for public information as in former years. Publicity is the only effectual check on the expenditures; and how a fit of economy seized certain parties so as not to print these accounts at a moment when the largest and most extraordinary expenditures had been and were being made which had ever occurred during the whole history of the University, is itself worthy of enquiry. But this much is certain, there were at the end of 1856 nearly seven thousand pounds which the 54th Section of the University Act places, not at the disposal of the Senate of the University, but at the disposal of the *Parliament* alone. The income Fund of the University for 1857 was reported at £15,000; but to what extent that has been since diminished by the enormous absorption of the capital of the fund for buildings, &c., we have no means of ascertaining. But more on this point when, in another paper, we come to speak of the general and various expenditures which have been made since the passing of the University Act.

At present let us look at the "current expenses" of University College only, and we will see how greatly they also have been increased since the passing of the University Act, while, as we purpose to show in a future paper, the standard of University

education has been actually lowered and the labours of the professors very considerably reduced, though their salaries have been largely increased; they having more than one third of the year for vacation, and labouring more than two months *less* each year than the Professors of Harvard College in the United States. We shall confine our references to the *Faculty of Arts*, as the Act does not allow any Faculty of Law or Medicine in University College. We learn from Returns laid before Parliament that, in 1845, when complaints were rife against the expenditures and monopoly of the late King's College, that the expenses of the Faculty of Arts were £2,564. In 1850, (after the passing of the University Act of 1849) they were £3,350. In 1853, (in April of which the present University Act was passed,) the expenses of the Faculty of Arts, including at the rate of £1400 per annum for four additional Professors, and £505 for a Registrar, Librarian, and Servants, amounted to £4,497. In 1857, the salaries of the several Professors and other officers are not given in the Public Accounts, but they are given in gross at £7,670—£3,173 more than they were in 1853. There are, however, two items of expense in this large sum not included in the expenses of 1853. The one is the salary of £200 per annum created for the Vice-Chancellor in 1854, and which Mr. Langton has received since 1856 in addition to his salary as Auditor of Public Accounts. The other item of expense is that of *Examiners*,—a new expense also created in 1854, amounting in 1854 to £360, and in 1856 to £540. The balance of the expenditure of 1857 over that of 1853, was for increase and arrears of increase of salaries.

In former times the Professors examined students as a part of their duty, and their compensation for which was included in their salary. Under the new economy, each Professor receives £20 a year as *examiner*, in addition to his largely increased salary. In 1856, one degree was conferred in Medicine, and the compensation to five Medical Examiners was £100. The number of other graduates was *six;* and the amount of compensation to Examiners was, as given above from the Parliamentary Returns, £540. At least an equal sum was paid for the same purpose in 1857, and also in 1858. Eleven of the Examiners were Professors in the University College—receiving each £20 per annum for the examination of their own students, in addition to their salaries,—in all £220.

The partnership business between the Toronto University and Toronto University College, works very conveniently for the various parties concerned. There is a College Fund, and a University Fund. The Librarian, Registrar, Library, Museum, &c., appertain nominally to the University; and when anything permanent or costly is required for the College, it is set down to the

rs of the profes-
aries have been
hird of the year
s *less* each year
ed States. We
rts, as the Act
ne in University
rliament that, in
iditures and mo-
:s of the Faculty
ig of the Univer-
53, (in April of
e expenses of the
)0 per annum for
strar, Librarian,
he salaries of the
en in the Public
—£3,173 more
er, two items of
xpenses of 1853.
ted for the Vice-
us received since
c Accounts. The
-a new expense
), and in 1856 to
57 over that of
salaries.

ents as a part of
included in their
r receives £20 a
ased salary. In
d the compensa-
The number of
compensation to
nentary Returns,
same purpose in
niners were Pro-
£20 per annum
ddition to their

o University and
eniently for the
und, and a Uni-
ty, Museum, &c.,
anything perma-
set down to the

amount of the *University* Fund; and when any officer of the College does anything as an Examiner, &c., in behalf of the University, he receives special compensation for it out of the University Fund. Thus the Professors, as members of the College Council one day, and of the Senate of the University next day, having two funds at their disposal, and without any of the responsibility that devolves upon heads of public departments, are most agreeably situated. And it is not surprising that they should therefore insist that the University and the College "are, and must be one institution." These two institutions and this double system fused into one, are as much at variance with the letter and spirit of the University Act, as they are opposed to sound economy, and to the best interests of the Province. It makes excellent times for its promoters, however hard the times may be in the country, and for general academical education; and its inventors have been known to exult at the manner in which they have been able to forestall the supporters of other colleges, and leave no surplus "to be appropriated by Parliament for Academical Education in Upper Canada." Their writers have haughtily sneered at, and assailed by name those whom they supposed were opposed to their "double shuffle" system. They have, therefore, no claim for reserve or indulgence at our hands in this discussion.

We maintain it to be a violation of one of the most important maxims of good government and political economy, for a Senate, or Council, or Board, having the control of public moneys, to be composed of persons who have a direct or indirect interest in the application of those moneys. A man is not allowed to sit in a jury on a case in which he has a personal interest; and it is as unBritish as it is unwise, that a permanent corporation having the control of vast sums of public money, should be composed of men who, (however competent and able in other respects,) have directly or indirectly, large personal interests in its expenditure. This has been a most serious evil complained of and sought to be remedied in the management of the University Funds from the beginning; and never was that evil more rife than since the passing of the University Act in 1853. This will appear more evident, when, in our next paper we discuss the general and various expenditures connected with the University College, Upper Canada College, and the Scholarship system—*sixty* Scholarships of £30 per annum each, having been in the Faculty of Arts alone, when there were not forty students in that Faculty in University College.

In the meantime, on the points to which we have referred, and as far as we have proceeded, we think every reader will agree that the Memorial of the Wesleyan Conference is fully justified in asking for Parliamentary investigation and interference.

PROOFS AND ILLUSTRATIONS NO. 4.

Recapitulation—Misquotations and misrepresentations of the *Christian Messenger* and Montreal *Witness* adduced and exposed—Methodist plan of a Provincial University and Superior Education—The *Leader's* argumentation—Three reasons why the Wesleyan Conference has originated the present appeal to the country and to the Legislature.

In our last paper we showed how the declared intentions and express provisions of the University Act have been disregarded and violated in the expenditure of University funds. We have also shown that the reported current expenses of Toronto University College have been nearly increased one hundred per cent. since the passing of the University Act of 1853, and almost three hundred per cent. since 1845, when loud complaints were made against the economy and justice of its management. We were next to notice generally the expenditures connected with Upper Canada College, University College, and the Scholarship system; but we must so far depart from our prescribed order of remark as to devote this paper chiefly to correct some gross misrepresentations which two professedly religious journals have made against the Wesleyan Conference on this subject. We allude to the Toronto *Christian Messenger* and the Montreal *Witness* —the former aspiring to be the organ of the Baptist denomination—the latter aspiring to be the organ of all Protestant denominations, but a most insidious and unscrupulous enemy of Wesleyan Methodism—ever with a Joab's salutation of " brother" on his lips, but ever with a Joab's sword concealed to thrust Methodism under the fifth rib as opportunity offers. The *Messenger* and *Witness* have both withheld from their readers the Memorial of the Conference; but they both *profess* to quote the prayer of that Memorial, and then make their comments and appeals upon it accordingly. Yet they both by *mutilation* falsify the prayer of the Memorial, and on their own deliberate misrepresentations found calumnious imputations and appeals against the Wesleyan Conference. The *Messenger* professes to state the prayer and objects of the Conference Memorial, and the *Witness* copies the *Messenger's* article, adding a *heading* of his own in the following words: " The essential unfairness of the Methodist Conference plan of College Reform;" and then employs the following words in an *editorial* reference to it: " We request our Methodist friends to read the article on our first page, copied from the *Christian Messenger*, and then say if they are willing as Protestants to carry on an agitation to endow two Roman Catholic and one Puseyite College, in order to get their own endowed? Also, if they

are willing as just men, to ask for the endowment of colleges of four or five religious denominations, and then shut out all others?" The *Messenger* presents the prayer and objects of the Memorial as follows: " Let us glance for a moment at the proposed reform advocated by the Methodist Conference. They pray the Legislature to pass an Act ' by which all the colleges now established in Upper Canada may be placed upon an equal footing—on equal terms in regard to public aid.' There are now eight colleges in Upper Canada, and, according to the prayer of the Conference, they are to be equal sharers in the college endowment on equal terms.' After animadverting on these colleges, the *Messenger* proceeds thus: " Then there is another view which may be taken of the prayer of the Conference. The prayer is, that ' colleges' now existing should be put upon ' equal footing.' What, then, is to become of the smaller and feebler bodies, which have as yet, no colleges so-called? Surely if strong bodies like the Methodist, Old Kirk, Free Kirk, and Episcopalians should receive Government aid, much more should feeble bodies, who have been, as yet, unable to get the length of a ' college,' receive a helping hand. But the Conference has not prayed for any such." Then the *Messenger* makes a piteous appeal on this gross illiberality and injustice of the prayer of the Conference.

Such are the statements and imputations of the Toronto *Messenger* and the Montreal *Witness*. Now it is our painful duty to show that the journals, in order to support a bad cause and assail the Conference, have deliberately mutilated the prayer of its Memorial, and *suppressed* in their quotations that very part of the prayer which they impugn the Conference for not making! They declare that the Conference shuts out of its prayer and its plan all except the colleges now existing. *The reverse is the fact,* as the prayer of the Memorial *not garbled,* will show. It is as follows:

" We therefore pray your Honourable House to cause an investigation to be instituted as to the manner in which the University Act has been administered, and the funds of the University and Upper Canada College have been expended, the immense advantage and benefit to the country of several competing colleges over the deadening and wasteful monopoly of one College, and cause an Act to be passed by which all the colleges now established, OR WHICH MAY BE ESTABLISHED in Upper Canada, may be placed on equal footing—on equal terms in regard to public aid, either as so many co-ordinate university colleges, or (which we think the best system) as so many colleges of one University."

The above five important words in capitals are omitted in the quotations of the *Messenger* and the *Witness ;** and on their own

---

* It is said the *Leader* first omitted these words, and the *Messenger* copied from him.

mutilation they impugn the motives and proceedings of the Conference,—an unfairness and dishonesty such as could hardly be exceeded by the Jesuitism which they profusely denounce, or by any reckless a print of political party. In another part of the Montreal *Witness*, the Methodist plan of giving public aid to colleges is objected to, because "the youths trained in such a State-endowed institution are likely to acquire a deep rooted predilection for governmental patronage!" The colleges and academies in the State of New York, denominational or otherwise, receive State aid according to their works; but is there an American so idiotic as to say that youths educated in such institutions thereby become the sycophants of Government? Our Grammar and Common Schools are all endowed to some extent by the State; but are the youths educated in them thus corrupted by State patronage? Or would the youth be more corrupted, if the schools were endowed by the State to twice the extent they now are? It requires such sages as the Toronto *Messenger* and Montreal *Witness* to see State corruption instead of national civilization, in this system. And singular to say; these very partizans advocate the State endowment of one college independent of all voluntary effort whatever, and that all the liberally educated youth of Upper Canada shall obtain their education at the "State-endowed institution!" Thus the common sense and consistency of the *Messenger* and *Witness* in argument are on a par with their fairness in statement in their onslaught upon the Conference.

The Methodist plan is to place aid to colleges upon the same footing as aid to common schools—each institution aided, not by the patronage or at the pleasure of any political man or party, but upon defined principles of law, according to the average attendance of pupils in prescribed branches of education; so that the religious denominations would be encouraged to become co-workers with the State and with each other in educating the country, and be no more dependent on party or government than are the trustees and supporters of any common school. The *Messenger* and *Witness* must know, that with the London University are affiliated not merely institutions popularly colleges, but such as are designated academies, seminaries, institutes, and even schools—each of which is as legally and fully recognized as is the University or King's College in London. By the Methodist plan, the University endowment would be just as much increased by the development of individual, municipal and denominational effort, and the corresponding diffusion of superior education, as is the Legislative Common School Grant increased by local effort and the diffusion of common school education. But such a system of comprehension and expansion transcends the contracted vision of Toronto mo-

nopolist advocates. One school is their measure of supply for Upper Canada; and a one college monopoly is their notion of a national system of superior education! On the other hand, the Methodist plan, while it is the London University system (and not that of New York State), in having one competent and impartial authority to fix and maintain a national standard of superior education, is the New York State system in the diffusion of superior as well as of elementary education and in encouraging all denominations and parties to train up as many youth as possible of all classes to that standard. Such a system is worthy of being called national, is based on national interests, and is fraught with national blessings; while the one college monopoly system is a burlesque upon the term national, is based on local and sectional interests, and is a perversion and abuse of national liberality.

The *Leader* has not descended to the petty larceny garbling and misrepresentation of the *Messenger* and *Witness* on this subject; but, with his usual quantum of pedantic sneering, the *Leader* excels them in the peculiar originality of his argumentation. He thinks it inadmissable to go to the preamble and provisions of an Act of Parliament ten or twelve years old to learn what was intended by, and what ought to be a University and Collegiate system for Upper Canada. The *Leader* is somewhat astray in his chronology, as he is awry in his law. The University Act is only half of twelve years old; but had it attained even the patriarchal age of twelve years, we doubt whether that would render obselete either its preamble or its enactments. The provisions of an Act of Parliament, as the revelations of a higher law, may be very repugnant to the feelings of so great a lover of liberty as the *Leader;* but we cannot yet dispense with such vulgar aids for the security of either property or rights. The *Leader* and his college patrons are no doubt shocked as well as surprised at so early a resurrection of a legal preamble and provisions which they had buried alive, and which they had fondly hoped would elude all future research under the monumental basis of a gigantic monopoly. They now complain that the Wesleyan Conference has dug up and revived these strangled and sepulchered provisions of the law, and has not waited for discoveries and action from other quarters to the same effect. Our answer to this is threefold. First, the Conference acts out its principles at its own time and in its own way, and leaves others to do the same. *Second*, the Conference assumed that the intentions and provisions of the University Act would be honourably and impartially carried into effect, as it knew that the University Endowment would soon be sufficient to constitute a growing fund for the promotion of Academical education generally, besides defraying the current expenses of Uni-

versity College; and though there was ground to apprehend that the Senate of the University was not proceeding in the spirit of the University Act, the Conference could not act upon suspicions and rumours. But at the very first annual meeting of Conference, after it had been clearly ascertained that the Provincial University was being converted into a one-college monopoly, its funds dissipated and reduced in an unprecedented manner, its surplus fund employed against the express provisions of the Act, thus extinguishing the last ray of hope of justice and nationality from the present University management, then, and not till then, did the Conference determine to bring the whole question before the country and the Legislature. Yet is there a *third* reason for the Conference taking an initiatory part in this proceeding. Its ministers and congregations are more numerous than those of any other religious persuasion in the country, and its Canadian history is that of a pioneer. It was the first to carry to the new settlers of Upper Canada the ministrations of religion, even before they had a regular constitution of Government. It was the first to establish missions among the Canadian heathen; the first to erect by voluntary effort a Seminary of learning in the country, and then to establish and open that Seminary as a University College. The Conference was also the first to advocate the cause of equal rights and privileges among all classes of inhabitants. More than thirty years ago, and for years until they achieved success, were the Methodists the only organized body whose ministers and members boldly, in the papers, by meetings and conventions, advocated the rights of the members of each religious persuasion to hold ground in which to bury their dead, and on which to build their Churches, and to be married, as well as be baptized and buried, by their own Ministers. The same may be said in regard to the Clergy Reserve question during many years. Though in the setttlement of that question, the principles of equal rights upon equal terms, originated and advocated by the Conference, were in a great measure secured, the object of the Conference advocacy to apply the proceedings of the Clergy Reserves to *educational purposes* was not realized. Had it been, Upper Canada would at this hour stand at the head of all countries in the world, in the amplitude of its public endowments for the education of its youth, with scarcely a tax or a fee from the primary school up to the University. It is therefore fitting that the Conference should take an initiary part in a movement to rectify wrong, to arrest extravagance, to destroy monopoly, and secure equal rights and advantages upon equal terms for all classes in regard to superior education. The *Leader* may sneer, and the *Messenger* and *Witness* may misrepresent and assail; but of the result in less than five years we have not a

shadow of doubt. The Conference now, as in former years, acts irrespective of political men or parties; it leaves slaveship to men and parties to such publications as the *Messenger* and *Witness* and their abettors, its appeals are to the conscience, justice and patriotism of every honest man of every sect or party, as its sole object is the attainment of the equal rights and the promotion of the best educational interests of all classes in the country. And in future years, the Conference will be acknowledged as great a benefactor to the country for having originated the present movement for freedom and equal justice in Academical education, as even its enemies now admit it to have been in battling alone for years in favour of freedom and equal justice among all denominations to hold grounds for graveyards, Churches, and Parsonages, and to have the solemnization of matrimony by their own ministers.

PROOFS AND ILLUSTRATIONS, NO. 5.

Expenditures connected with Upper Canada College, the University, University College and Scholarships—Contrast between the London and Toronto Universities as to expenditures, Buildings, and Scholarships—Extravagance, injustice and folly of the Toronto University, Grammar School, College and Scholarship Systems exposed.

Having corrected certain misrepresentations respecting the character and objects of the Wesleyan Conference remonstrance and memorial, we now proceed to justify its complaints as to the expenditures generally connected with Upper Canada College, the University, University College, and the Arts Scholarship system.

1. *Upper Canada College.* When this institution was established in 1829, there was no University or University College in Upper Canada, and it was designed to impart the highest education the country could afford. In this capacity, and under its earlier management, it did good service; but for some twenty years its whole work has been that of a Common and Grammar School. It teaches no higher or other subjects than those included in the programmes for Grammar and Common Schools; and while other Grammar Schools are not permitted to teach the Elementary subjects of Common School instruction, and thus swell the number of their pupils at the expense of the

Common Schools, Upper Canada College possesses the peculiar privilege of doing the work of the Common School as well as of the Grammar School. Yet in no respect has it presented a model for either Common or Grammar Schools; but the irregularities and pernicious moral influences associated with it, together with its enormous expenditures, were long matters of serious and loud complaint. Those pupils who escaped the contagion of vice during their attendance at the College, and who have subsequently distinguished themselves in useful professions and employments, owe to home influences rather than to the atmosphere of the College, the elements of character to which they are most indebted for their success. Latterly, we believe some improvement has taken place, and especially, as we understand, since the introduction into the College of the spirit and rules of discipline of the Model Grammar School for Upper Canada. But Toronto has its Grammar and Common Schools as well as other cities and towns, and where is the necessity or equity of a united Common and Grammar School under the imposing but inappropriate name of " Upper Canada College ?" The necessity is, of course, simply that of the fifth wheel to a carriage. If Toronto defrayed the expenses of this Supplementary Institution, there could be no objection to it; but when it is done at the expense of the country at large, and especially of the Grammar Schools of the country, the case is very different. Were the proceeds of the lands and moneys lavished on Upper Canada College bestowed for the benefit of the Grammar Schools of the country at large,—a first class Grammar School, as efficient as that of Upper Canada College itself, could be established in nearly every county of Upper Canada.

Then look at results. First, as to the contribution of Students to the University. The names of the Schools from which the Students have come, who have matriculated in the University, have been improperly withheld from the public; but we have the names of the Schools in which Students have been educated who have, in 1858 and 1859, attained scholarships at their Matriculation Examinations. In 1858, the pupils of Upper Canada College obtained one of these Scholarships out of eight. The other seven Scholarships were, with one exception, obtained by pupils of other Grammar Schools. In 1859, of nine Scholarships in the Faculty of Arts, of the first year, the pupils of the Upper Canada College, according to the Official Report, obtained only one; the other eight having being obtained by pupils from other Grammar Schools. At a recent Convocation the President of University College, stated that " Of the first class Honors distributed at Matriculation, eight were obtained by pupils of Upper Canada College, seven by

those of Galt Grammar School, three by the pupils of Barrie Grammar School; two by those of London Grammar School, and two were self-taught." While of the two Examiners, one was a late Principal of Upper Canada College, and the other one, of the present Masters, (an advantage in competing Examinations which Upper Canada College has usually enjoyed,) it will be seen that Upper Canada College is only a shade above the Galt Grammar School; though the latter received only £150 public aid, and the former £5,897! Then as to the number of pupils. This ought to be enormously large, as the College is a Union Grammar and Common School. It has, we understand, declined nearly one third during the last two years. But even at the largest, the attendance of pupils at Upper Canada College, is less that at the corresponding united Grammar and Common Schools of Brantford or Hamilton. And if the Common School pupils in Upper Canada College be abstracted from the Grammar School pupils [as required by law in regard to the Grammar Schools,] the attendance of pupils at Upper Canada College, with its enormous public endowments and grants at the expense of the other Grammar Schools of the Province, will be found actually less than at the Grammar Schools in Hamilton, St. Catherines, Belleville, and in several other places, and far less than in the Grammar School department of Victoria College.

Further, look at the public expenditure in support of this Toronto Union Common and Grammar School, called "Upper Canada College." We cannot enter into details; but by returns laid before Parliament down to December, 1857, the sum of £129,633 15s. 2d. had been expended in behalf of Upper Canada College, besides £4,581 2s. 2d. invested in buildings. From the returns laid before Parliament in 1856, we copy the following items:

"Expenditure for Upper Canada College, as shown by the Annual Account was as follows:

Paid from Income Fund.................£6,291 16s 5d
Paid from Permanent Fund per Repairs to
 Buildings, per order in Council......... 2,149 4 11

Total expenditure per U. C. College for all
 purposes during the year 1855.........£8,441 1 4

We can find no returns of the expenditures of U. C. College in 1852. The Salaries of Masters for 1850, 1851, and 1853, was £7,505; the Salaries of Masters under the present management, during the last three years reported [1855, 1856, 1857,]

3

is £10,089. The total expenditures of U. C. College for 1850, 1851, and 1853, was £12,974; the total expenditures in support of the same United Common and Grammar Schools during the years 1855, 6, and 7, are £27,841; that is, £14,867 more than during the three years preceding the inauguration of the present management. Though our prescribed brevity does not permit us to enter into detail, we cannot forbear noting two items in account with the Permanent Fund for 1857. The one is, "Amount appropriated for addition to Boarding House," £2,629. The other item is, "amount appropriated for alterations to Masters' houses, play-grounds, racket-court," &c., £2,000. Thus when the Income Fund, increased by Parliamentary grants, and grants in the form of loans from the University Fund, is not sufficient to meet the views of the managers of U. C. College, the *Permanent* Fund is appropriated, and the Income Fund thereby proportionately reduced. The maxim, "seize the *treasures* of the present day," seems to be acted upon, leaving posterity as well as the other Grammar Schools of Upper Canada, to take care of themselves.

Such is the expenditure by the Senate in support of its one Grammar School—the counter part of its expenditure in building up a one College monopoly. The average School Income Fund of the 75 Grammar Schools in U. C., during the last three years, was £7,186 per annum—total £21,558—not so much by £6,293 as the Senate has expended during the last three years reported on its one Grammar School, though more pupils are taught in each of some of these starved country Grammar Schools, than in the Senate's favoured Grammar School, and though from each of some of them are sent as many Students to the University as from Upper Canada College. These facts are trumpet-tongued in showing the injustice, the impolicy, the extravagance and folly of the Senate's sytem in building up its one Grammar School. Had no other Grammar Schools been established and endowed in the country, we would doubtless have as loud a monopolist cry against the proposal to establish and endow them as we now have against the endowment of more than one College. We would be told, how adequate is Upper Canada College with its 13 Masters and large endowment and grants and loans, to impart Grammar School education to all the youth of Upper Canada able to acquire it. But facts contradict this theory. Facts show that some of the citizens of Toronto prefer sending their children away to country Grammar Schools, rather than keep them at home at the Upper Canada College; and facts show that while Upper Canada College has latterly exceeded the whole 75 Grammar Schools of Upper Canada in its consumption of public endowments, it is equalled

by several of them separately in their contributions of Students to the Classes of the University and the amount and quality of instruction to pupils. The folly of the abortive attempt to have one mammoth endowed Grammar School, instead of a large number of moderately endowed competing Grammar Schools—all required to perform certain work, and to work up to a prescribed standard—it is only equalled by the folly of having one State endowed College to the exclusion of all others. The whole system is essentially rotten, unjust and unpatriotic, and is a wasteful misapplication of the resources of the country for academical education. This will appear still more obvious when we consider,

II. The expenditures connected with the Toronto University, and University College in Toronto. The President of the University College has recently declared that the University and College were and must be "one Institution." In the first of these papers, we showed the absurdity of this assumption, its inconsistency with the English use of the term University and College, and its contradiction to the avowed intentions and express provisions of our University Act itself. The Senate admitted the distinction between the two institutions, when in its report for 1856, it said—"the University of Toronto and University College are *distinct institutions*, and have separate functions." Also in the University returns for 1857, laid before Parliament in 1858, under the head of "University College Toronto," we have the following statement to the same effect. "Another Provincial Statute, whereby important modifications were effected, and the designation was changed from 'King's College' to that of 'Universtiy of Toronto' came into operation on January 1st, 1850. Under this Statute the establishment was conducted until April, 1853, when the the University was *divided* into *two* Institutions, one retaining the title of the University of Toronto, and the other styled University College, Toronto. The first of these institutions is formed *on the model of the University of London*, its functions being limited to prescribing subjects of examination for degrees, scholarships, prizes, or certificate of honors, examining candidates therein, and conferring such degrees or distinction."

Here it is clearly admitted that the University and University College are two distinct institutions, and that it was the very object of the Act of 1853, in contradistinction of that of 1850, to make them two distinct institutions with separate functions; but, as we have shown in the *third* of these papers, it has been the object of the Senate to make them one Institution, and the President of University College, at its last convocation, suppos-

ing that the work was now sufficiently consolidated for avowal, openly and as he said, advisedly, declares that the University and University College are and must " be one Institution !" and the monopolist advocates are instructed, to represent the Wesleyan Conference as striving to pull down a Provincial University, because it opposes the monopoly of University College, though it declares itself in favour of a Provincial University and in favour of the objects of the University Act of 1853.

From the admissions in the above extracts of the Senate's own reports, as well as from the preamble and clauses of the Act, our University was to be founded on the model of the London University, and with its functions, which are simply and solely those of an authoritative examining Board. The Act expressly guards against our University having any professorship or teachership of any kind whatever.

The question then is, what need of a building, Museum, &c., for an examining Board? All the accommodation it requires is a place for its own meetings, and rooms for the examination of students twice a-year. The County Boards of Public Instruction meet at least twice a year, and any one of them examines more candidates, and gives more certificates than does the Senate of the University. The London University does the same; and so does the Queen's University in Ireland. But has the British Parliament permitted a sixpence to be expended for the erection of a London University, or a Queen's University? Several Colleges of Queen's University have been erected in Ireland; and many colleges are affiliated to the London University. But the Queen's University, though it prescribes the course of studies for the colleges connected with it, as well as examines their students for degrees and certificates, occupies only two or three rooms in Dublin Castle, (the Government House,) for its meetings and the examination of students as they come up for examination for certificates and degrees twice a year. And the London University occupies, with its registrar and clerk, two or three rooms in Somerset House, in the Strand—a building devoted to various offices of individuals and societies.

If then, no expensive building—indeed, no separate building whatever—was necessary for the Senate and duties of the Queen's University in Ireland, or of London University in England, where is the need of it for the Senate and duties of the Toronto University in Canada? Is the Senate of the Toronto University composed of greater men than the noblemen, bishops, and distinguished literary gentlemen who compose the Senates of the London and Queen's Universities? Is Upper Canada a

richer country than England? With all their wealth and greatness in the United Kingdom, they thought no expense necessary for the erection or purchase of buildings for either Queen's or London University, the latter of which was specified by statute as the model for Toronto University. We appeal to no vulgar feelings on this subject. We appeal to the example of the older and richer mother country. We appeal to the example of that very London University which is the legally prescribed model of the Toronto University, as we have appealed, in the third of those papers to the provisions of the University Act, which expressly limits expenditures to current expenses and the repairs and improvements of the present buildings. Yet have these buildings (though almost new) been abandoned, and contrary to the example of the London University, and the provisions of our own Act, have new and expensive buildings been erected, under the pretext of accommodating both the University and University College.

In their report for 1856 the Senate acknowledge the sum of £75,000 "for buildings out of the Permanent Fund!" that is out of the capital of the Endowment—thereby reducing the *annual* income *forever* to the amount of the interest on that sum. How this sum has been expended, or what additional sums have been expended, we have no means of judging. The auditor of the accounts is also the Vice-Chancellor of the University, on whose recommendation, and under whose oversight, all these expenditures have been made. Nothing more is known by the public since 1857, when these extraordinary expenditures were commenced; and the accounts for 1857 are given chiefly in gross, not in detail. The Senate, in their Report for 1856, admit "that such a large sum [£75,000] abstracted from the capital, together with that devoted to the increase of the library and museum, will make a serious deduction from the University Income Fund; whilst there is little doubt that the occupation of more extensive buildings, and the maintenance of the grounds in connexion with them, will entail increased expenditure." Here is the confessed policy of diminishing income, and increasing current expenditure—a man impoverishing his family to build and maintain a fine house—the reduction of the means of academic education in the country to the amount of between twenty and thirty thousand dollars a-year in order to have a fine building in Toronto!

The ordinary expenditures in support of this amalgamation of institutions, seems to be little less remarkable than these extraordinary expenditures. An examination of details would show this in various particulars; but we must limit ourselves to a few items. In reply to an address of the Legislative Assembly

for a specific returns for 1855, (long before the erection of the new buildings was commenced,) the Bursar, while he replies that the "Total expenditure for Upper Canada College for all purposes during the year 1855, was £8,441 1s. 4d.," replies that the "Total amount paid on account of the University of Toronto last year, [1855] or appropriated to purposes connected with the University College, including Joint Management, as shown by the annual account, was £14,664 6s. 8d.

The Bursar reports the expenditure in connection with the University and College for 1856, (including £1,687 on account of building appropriation,) to have been £18,963 14s. 5d., besides £6,611 3s. 7d. in connexion with Upper Canada College.

In 1857 the Bursar reports the expenditure connected with Upper Canada College to have been £7,541 2s. 8d., with University College, £13,978 19s. 8d., besides £3,287 11s. 1d. for the Library and Museum, £26,037 4s. 4d. on account of new buildings. These are the last returns printed. Such facts will only be weakened by comment. Every candid reader's own judgment and feelings will furnish ample comment upon such unparalleled increase and extravagance of expenditure in behalf of one Grammar School and one College, to the permanent reduction of income, and to the wrong of Grammar Schools and academical institutions throughout Upper Canada. According to the returns, down to the end of 1857, the sum of £317,914 7s. 4d. had been expended in connection with Toronto University—a fact as melancholy as it is almost incredible.

III. It remains to say a few words on the *Arts Scholarship system*—designed, as it has exclusively proved, a means of increasing the students at University College. A statute passed by the Senate in 1854, provides, "That sixty scholarships, of the value of thirty pounds each, be established for the encouragement and assistance of under-graduates in the Faculty of Arts; ten in the Faculty of Medicine; and five in each of the Departments of Civil Engineering and Agriculture, in addition to ten in the Faculty of Law, which have been already established by Statute passed by the Senate." At the time of passing this statute, there were, according to the official Report, *twenty eight* students in the Faculty of Arts in University College, and in the following year, *thirty-six*. Yet that year the scholarships in the Faculty of Arts were increased to *seventy*—keeping up the proportion of two scholarships for every student in the College. It is natural to suppose that from such an abundant seed of scholarships a large crop of scholars at University College would be produced. This has been the case,

[left column — partial, page edge cut off]

e erection of the
vhile he replies
la College for all
ls. 4d.," replies
he University of
rposes connected
Management, as
5s. 8d.

nnection with the
1,687 on account
,963 14s. 5d., be-
r Canada College.

re connected with
2s. 8d., with Uni-
£3,287 11s. 1d.
4d. on account of
rinted. Such facts
ry candid reader's
ple comment upon
e of expenditure in
College, to the per-
vrong of Grammar
out Upper Canada.
of 1857, the sum of
connection with To-
s it is almost incre-

he *Arts Scholarship*
oved, a means of in-
e. A statute passed
sixty scholarships, of
shed for the encour-
es in the Faculty of
d five in each of the
griculture, in addition
been already estab-
At the time of pass-
the official Report,
rts in University Col-
. Yet that year the
increased to *seventy*—
hips for every student
se that from such an
p of scholars at Uni-
is has been the case.

Yet the thing was so overdone, and so beyond what could be decently disposed of, that we believe the number of scholarships in Arts has been made fifty—or about one scholarship per student.

Now in the London University, with its numerous affiliated colleges, and which was to be the model for the Toronto University, and where there was no plan to build up one college at the expense of all others, the Senate has established in the Faculty of Arts, one scholarship each year in classics, and one in Mathematics and Natural Philosophy at matriculation, at £30 each, and tenable for two years; and one of £50 in classics, and one in Mathematics and Natural Philosophy at taking the degree of B. A., and tenable for three years. Also one scholarship in Jurisprudence at taking the degree of LL. B., and one in each department of the Faculty of Medicine. The contrast, therefore, between the London University and the Toronto University in respect to scholarships is as marked as it is in respect to expenditures for buildings. And we omit altogether for the sake of brevity the almost numberless prizes which have been instituted at Toronto in addition to the scholarships. In the London University all is economy and quiet dignity, in the Toronto University all is lavish expenditure and gaudy show.

In concluding this paper we remark—

1. That though we have referred to the Senate, we have reason to believe that few members except the salaried Vice Chancellor and those connected with University and Upper Canada Colleges, know much or anything of most of the e penditures which we have quoted from the official return Many of the items will probably be as new to them as to others.

2. That the system which has led to this enormous expenditure and loss of educational funds is radically bad in itself, and therefore cannot be mended, but must be changed. Each succeeding act in the drama of Toronto University and College reform has invariably been followed by increased prodigality and waste; and will continue to be so as long as the false system is continued. In a future paper it will be our duty to demonstrate the falsity, the injustice, the unsuitableness to the country of the whole system.

In the meantime, the facts already adduced abundantly justify the complaints in the Memorial of the Wesleyan Conference on the score of expenditures, and the appeal for parliamentary investigation and reform.

PROOFS AND ILLUSTRATIONS, NO. 6.

Objects of a Provincial University—Threefold Argument against the Toronto System stated—A four fold answer to an objection—Present Standard of admission to University College shown to be much lower than that of 1852, before the passing of the University Act, and a full year's work lower than that of Harvard College, near Boston, while the *work* during the four year's course of study is an Academical year less than that of Harvard College—Teaching of Grammar School, Theological Students in Toronto, a reason for reducing the University College course of instruction.

We now proceed to justify that part of the Memorial of the Wesleyan Conference which says:—"The curriculum of the University studies, instead of being elevated and conformed to that of the London University, has been revised and changed three times since 1853, and reduced by options and otherwise, below what it was formerly, and below what it is in the English Universities, and below what it is in the best Colleges in the United States."

Any one who will compare the curriculum of University studies in the Faculty of Arts prescribed by the Senate in 1854, 1857, and 1858, will find each differing from the other; and curriculums in the Faculties of Law and Medicine have undergone like variations. But we confine our remarks chiefly to the Faculty of Arts, as that is the only Faculty allowed by law in University College.

The argument for a Provincial University, and against various university colleges, is, that the former will maintain an elevated standard of University education, and by its examinations, independent of all colleges, give value to University degrees, while various university colleges will let down the standard of university education and confer degrees on partial examinations and without regard to merits or attainments, and therefore without value. The University Act was expressly intended to accomplish the above averred objects of a Provincial University.

Now, if it be shown that the course of studies in the Faculty of Arts in the University of Toronto is not even equal to what it was in 1852, and that it has been actually reduced instead of being elevated since the passing of the University Act in 1853, then will the great objects of that Act be proved to have been defeated, the argument for a

Provincial University in contradistinction to several university colleges, be proved to have been thus far falsified, and the vast expenditures in connection with one college be proved to have been an unjust and useless waste of public money. In proof of what is here intimated, and in justification of the complaint of the Wesleyan Conference, we will examine, *First,* The standard of matriculation in the University now and before, as well as after, the passing of the Act of 1853; *Secondly,* the nature and effects of the options and exemptions in reducing the course of studies and the standard of qualifications for degrees contrary to the example of the London University and the best American Colleges; *Thirdly,* the system of appointing Examiners and the modes of examinations, contrary to those of the London and other English Universities, as also of the best American Colleges.

1. *First,* The standard of matriculation in the Toronto University now and before, as well as after the passing of the Act in 1853.

But here we must anticipate and answer an objection. It may be said that the undergraduate course was formerly *three* years, but that it is now *four* years, and if the standard of matriculation is lower than it was formerly, the period of study is longer. To this objection we return a four-fold answer: 1. Though the undergraduate course has been extended from three to four years, the terms during each of those years have been reduced from three to two; and the two terms occupy less time than did the three terms: so that, although the period of the course has been lengthened, the time of labor during that period has been very little increased. 2. Though the course has been prolonged, the amount of labor during that course has been reduced rather than increased—as will hereafter appear; so that, as more than one of the graduates have remarked, and as is notorious, a degree of B. A. in the University can be obtained with less labor now than it could be in former years. 3. The four year's course existed in 1855, (as the Return for that year, laid before Parliament in 1856, Appendix to Journals, No. 11, shows), and the reduction in the standard of matriculation was not made until 1857; 4. The undergraduate course in the best American colleges is four years; and in Harvard as well as other colleges, the labor during *each year* exceeds that of Toronto University College by *two months:* so that there are *eight* months [or more than a Toronto academic year] longer work by the professors and students in Harvard

University, than in the Toronto University, while, as we will presently show, the standard of matriculation is much higher in the former than in the latter, and the Toronto emasculating system of options and exemptions, is but sparingly allowed in Harvard, and not at all by the London University.

In returning to the question, we note first the standard of matriculation as it existed in 1852, before the passing of the present Act. From the Returns laid before Parliament in the Session of 1852-3, (Appendix L to the Journals) under the head of "Matriculation Examinations," we extract the following:—

"By a Statute by the Senate in 1851, the following have been appointed as the subjects of examination for candidates of admission:—

1852.

"CLASSICS, &c.—Homer, Illiad B. I.; Xenophon Anabasis, B. I.; Lucian, Charon and Vita; Virgil Æneid, B. VI.; Ovid, Fasti, B. I.; Cæsar de Bello Gall. Bb. V. and VI.; Translation from English into Latin Prose; English Composition; English History to the present time; Roman History to the accession of Augustus; Grecian History to the death of Alexander; Outlines of Ancient and Modern Geography.

"MATHEMATICS.—First Four Rules of Arithmetic; Vulgar and Decimal Fractions; Extraction of Square Root; First Four Rules of Algebra; Proportion and Progressions; Simple Equations; Euclid, B. I."

Then follows a list of books and subjects "additional for candidates for honours." And the subjects of the nine terms of the whole course compare favorably with those of the eight terms of the present course in the University. The standard of matriculation, as also the course of studies, was the same in 1853. In 1854, the whole course of study was revised by the Senate under the present Act. The result was laid before Parliament in 1855, and will be found in the Appendix M to the Journals for that year. The standard of matriculation, and the prescribed "Matriculation Examinations" were precisely the same as in 1852, except that in classics Ovid's Fasti, B. I., was omitted, and " or " was inserted before Lucian, and in Roman History Nero was substituted for Augustus.

Up to this time, therefore, though the tendency of pro-

ceedings was downward, the former Toronto University standard of matriculation was substantially maintained, in connection with the four year's undergraduate course.

In the Report for 1856, laid before Parliament in 1857, Appendix to Journals No. 28, it is said, "No alteration in the course of studies since last Report." But in 1857 (see Appendix No. 12 to Journals of Parliament for 1858) we have a new course of studies inferior to any which had preceded it in its standard of matriculation, and throughout, in consequence of options and exemptions. In the subjects for matriculation, those for mathematics, history, and geography were the same as those given above for 1852; but in classics we have the following:

"Xenophon, Anabasis, B. I., Sallust, Catalina; Translation from English into Latin prose."

Here are omitted from the same examination of former years, Homer, B. I.; Lucian, Charon and Vita; Cæsar, De Bello Gall., Bb.V. and VI.; Virgil, Æneid, B.VI; Ovid, Fasti, B. I;—two Greek and three Latin authors—about one year's work below the standard established before the passing of the University Act in 1853. In the University College for 1859, we observe another modification in the course of studies, and the sixth book of Virgil's Æneid added to the one book of Xenophon and Sallust's Cataline; but still nearly a year lower than that of 1852, or of 1855.

Let us now examine the requisites for admission, or the standard of matriculation in the best American colleges, and see how far we fall below them. We might select Columbia college, and Yale and Harvard; but for the sake of brevity, we will confine ourselves to the latter. The following are the subjects of examination for matriculation in Harvard University, as given in the catalogue of 1859-60:—

"LATIN DEPARTMENT.—The *whole* of Virgil; the *whole* of Cæsar's Commentaries; Cicero's Select Orations; Andrews and Stoddard's Latin Grammar, including Prosody; and in writing Latin.

"GREEK DEPARTMENT.—Felton's Greek Reader, or the *whole* of the Anabasis of Xenophon, and the first three books of the Iliad (omitting the catalogue of ships in the second book.) Sophocles' Greek Grammar, including Prosody; and in writing Greek with the accents.

"MATHEMATICAL DEPARTMENT.—Davies' Chases, or Eaton's Arithmetic; Euler's Algebra to the extraction of the Square

Root; and 'an introduction to Geometry and the Science of Form, prepared from the most approved Prussian Text Books.'

HISTORICAL DEPARTMENT.—Mitchell's Ancient and Modern Geography; Worcester's Elements of History.

The examination in Latin and Greek Grammars, in Latin and Greek composition, and in Arithmetic, Algebra and Geometry, is in writing; an hour being allowed to each exercise."

Such is the standard of matriculation in Harvard University of Massachusetts, where everything in education is known to be unpretentious, thorough, and practical; a standard more than a year's work in advance of that of the Toronto University.

It is therefore clear that the reverse of the objects of the University Act has resulted from the proceeding under it in regard to elevating the standard of University education, at least so far as the commencement of it is concerned; and we shall show that the process of it is, from its system of options and exemptions, as checkered and disjointed as its beginning is humble.

But before we do so, it is proper to enquire why the standard of admission to the University of Toronto has been so greatly reduced below its former self, and even below that of the Fourth Form of a Grammar School? One reason at least appears to be, the University College has been made the convenient instrument of promoting the objects of three Theological schools in Toronto, the students of which come up with the beginnings of a Grammar school education, and pursue it in University College, while they are attending Theological lectures under their own Professors. These "occasional students," or "students" (as they are technically called) are much more numerous than the regular students and undergraduates in the college; and in their behalf the College is thus made to do the work which the Grammar school programmes show may and ought to be done by the Grammar Schools. And yet the very parties who are thus using the teachings and getting the educational standard lowered of University College for denominational purposes, most lustily exclaim against denominational colleges! They employ a Provincial Endowment and a Provincial Non-denominational College to supply the Grammar School wants of their own denominational and even theological schools, and then oppose, as they say on principle, public aid to denominational col-

leges! Were ever action and profession more opposed to each other? It was long a subject of complaint and agitation that the University of King's College at Toronto was subservient to the interests of the Church of England; but was the Church of England as such driven out of it in order to convert King's College into a supplementary school for the theological institutes of the Presbyterian and the Congregationalist? Was that the object of the People and Legislature of Upper Canada in changing King's College into University, and then separating Toronto University from University College? In the days of alleged Church-of-England management, this much must be confessed, that the standard of admission to the University, and (as will appear in another paper) the standard of the whole University course was kept up so as to place every Canadian graduate upon a level with graduates of the English, or best American Universities. The standard of University admission and teaching was never until recently, made tributary to theological schools for students who, according to the system and standard of Ministerial education in Scotland, would be in the Grammar School rather than in the Divinity Hall. The necessities of Canada may require a different arrangement, but it ought not to be at the sole expense of the public. The candid, and just, and liberal members of the Presbyterian and Congregational Churches must see the inconsistency and absurdity of parties loudly opposing public aid to denominational colleges, while they themselves quietly make a publicly endowed college the grammar school of their own theological institutions for the education of their own clergy. And we submit to any impartial and intelligent man, whether it is not infinitely betterfor the highest educational as well as religious interests of the country that there should be denominational, as well as non-denominational colleges, competing and maintaining a high standard of education prescribed by Provincial authority, than a one University College let down to do grammar school work in order to advance the objects of denominational *theological* institutes?

We merely hint here at what admits of a large and thorough discussion; and we are prepared to meet the Toronto theological school advocates of a one college monopoly in regard to any aspect of the subject.

In the meantime, every father in Canada (however defective may be his own education) who incurs the expense of giving his son a University education, every young man who devotes his time and strength to acquire such an educa-

tion, and every man who truly wishes for the elevation of Canada, must desire that a Canadian University education, at its commencement, in its progress and at its completion, should be inferior to none in Great Britain or America. This is what our country requires and has a right to expect. We have shown what the Toronto University education has become at its commencement; and we purpose next to show that its progress and completion correspond with its beginning.

PROOFS AND ILLUSTRATIONS, NO. 7.

Objects of Collegiate Studies—Options and Exemptions during three out of the four years of the Toronto University College Course—their baneful tendency and effects—the classical pass-work, or required undergraduate classical studies of the first two years in Toronto University College in 1852 and 1859-60, and in Harvard College, compared—the Toronto classical first two years' course one half now what it was in 1852, and less than half that of Harvard and Yale Colleges compared with those of Toronto University College—effects of them contrasted—Academic year nine weeks longer, twelve hours more work per week, and more than twice the amount of professional instruction and assistance given to undergraduates at Harvard than at Toronto—Injustice of the Toronto system of college lectures to pass undergraduates, compared with the English and Harvard systems—Toronto University system of appointing Examiners and conducting Examinations of students the reverse of the University examination system of Old England and New England—Contrasts and Conclusion.

Having shown that the standard of matriculation, or of commencing the studies in the Toronto University College has been greatly lowered since the passing of the University Act in 1853, and is now a full year lower than in the best Colleges in the United States, we next proceed to consider the nature and effects of the system of options or exemptions in still further reducing the standard of these studies throughout their course. The great objects of collegiate studies intellectually considered, apart from religion and morals, are to develop the faculties of Language and Reason, and to form that intellectual discipline, without which there is no intellectual progress throughout life. An undisciplined mind is

often most potent in its first efforts: a disciplined mind increases in power as it grows in years until the decay of nature. Language is the expression of Reason; Reason moulds and directs the exercise of Language. To develop the Faculty of language, requires the study and exercise of language: and to develop the Faculty of Reason requires the investigation and practice of vigorous reasoning, proceeding from self-evident or certain truths, whether appertaining to numbers, forms, or quantities. To cultivate the essential and wonderful Faculty of Language, the study of the classic languages of ancient Greece and Rome is commended by the example of all Europe and America for centuries, as is the Geometry of the ancients for the best examples and exercise of perfect reasoning. By the study of the former, the student acquires the key of universal grammar, a familiarity with the most beautiful thoughts most beautifully expressed, an acquaintance with books which have connected generations and nations with each other, which have been recognized and studied for twenty centuries as models of eloquence and poetry, which have influenced the thoughts and language of many modern nations, and have furnished the finest examples and illustrations found in the productions of our greatest modern poets, orators, scholars, and historians. By the study of the latter, the mind is trained to habits of accurate thought and reasoning on which the intellectual progress and interests of life so much depend. Therefore in the best Colleges and Universities, the first and largest place has been given to study of classics and mathematics—to the former more than to the latter, as they involve both mental discipline and subjects which sympathise with the emotions and relations of social life. With these studies are associated those of the sciences with which men have to do and in which they are making progress from day to day, of civil polity, history, and literature, of mental and moral science—the laws of the human mind and the principles of human conduct.

These being objects of collegiate studies, the enquiry now is, how far the Toronto University College has maintained that standard of studies throughout its course which it formerly maintained, and which is regarded so essential by the practice of the best Universities in Europe and America? During the *first* year's course of studies there are no options or exemptions, except in regard to Hebrew (French and German are not included in the first year's course); but under the head of the *second* year's course of studies, we find the following in the College Calendar for 1859-1860:

"Undergraduates are not required to take *French*, *German* and *Hebrew*, but any one at their option.

"Candidates for honors in any department, who have also in the first year obtained University first-class honors, either in Greek *or*

Latin, *or* mathematics, *or* in both Modern Languages and Natural Sciences, are not required to take *any* branch in which they have passed the *University examination in the first year;* but such candidates having been only examined in pure mathematics in the first year, must also take applied Mathematics this year."

Here it will be seen that if a student obtains during the first year "first-class honors" in any of the various subjects enumerated, (no difficult matter,) and becomes a candidate for honors the second year, he is exempted from pursuing every subject in which he has passed an examination at all the first year! Then under the head of the *third* year's course of studies we have the following option and exemptions:

"Undergraduates are not required to take both *Greek and Latin*, and *French and German*, but either at their option. They may also omit *Hebrew, Chaldee* and *Italian*.

"Candidates for honors in any department, who have obtained University first-class honors in the second year, are not required to take in other departments more than two branches, in which they have been previously examined; and these branches may be selected by such candidates at their option!"

It will be here noted, that if a student has obtained first-class honors the second year, and is a candidate for honors the third year, he may omit all but two branches in connexion with in which he is a candidate for honors; that is, out of seven branches of the prescribed course (besides the modern and Oriental languages), the candidate for honors may select three; and this year embraces the most important part of the course in Mental Philosophy, History and Ethnology, Natural History, Chemistry, Mathematics and Natural Philosophy, Latin and Greek; and any undergraduate may omit both Latin and Greek, if he prefers French and German!

Finally, under the head of the fourth year's course of studies, we have the following list of exemptions and options:

"Undergraduates may take at their option either *Greek and Latin* or *French and German*, and also either *Mathematics and Natural Philosophy*, or *Organic Chemistry*, or *Geology and Physical Geography;* or *Meteorology*. The may also omit *Italian, Spanish, Hebrew, Chaldee, Syric and Arabic*.

"Candidates for honors in any department, who have also obtained Univerity first-class honors in the third year, are not *required to take any other department* than that in which they are candidates for honors.

"Such candidates for honors in *Modern Languages* are not required to take in addition to *English, French, German, Italian and Spanish*, but any three of them.

"Such candidates for honors in *Natural Sciences*, are not required to take *Chemistry, Natural History, and Mineralogy, Geology*, and *Physical Geography*, but any two at their option."

Thus any undergraduate may again omit *Latin and Greek*, and also *Mathematics;* and any student who has obtained first-class honors in the third year, and is a candidate for honors in the fourth year, may omit all the departments of study except one; and for the study of that one a thirty pounds scholarship is offered!

Such a number and variety of options and exemptions in a collegiate course of studies we have never before witnessed. It is perfectly clear, in such a system of almost endless options and exemptions, a degree of B. A. can have no definite signification, especially as applied to a man of honors. He may not have studied a word of Greek or Latin, or solved a problem in Algebra, or demonstrated a proposition of Geometry, after the first year of his course of studies, and yet be B. A. with honors! The more carefully one analyses the nature, working, and effects of these numerous options and exemptions, the more strongly must he feel that the course is a collection of miscellaneous lectures and exercises, rather than a systematic and symmetrical development and disciplinary training of the mind; that the wide field created for whim and fancy, and rendered attractive by numerous scholarships, leaves little room or hope (so far as the influence of the system is concerned) for the formation of those elements of character on which usefulness, greatness, happiness, and success most depend. It is not surprising that under the operations of such a system of taste and caprice, the able Professor of Mathematics in University College should feel sensible on being compelled to reduce rather than elevate his examination papers from year to year.

If we turn from this fancy field of honours and scholarships to the less enchanting one of *pass-work*, we see that while the honour man can leave his classics at the end of the first year, every undergraduate can abandon them at the end of the second year. In a previous paper we have seen how greatly the *classical* standard of matriculation has been reduced since 1852 and 1855; we will now show that the course of *classical* studies the two years only that undergraduates are required to pursue them, have been reduced beyond precedent and without parallel. These studies are about one-third less than they were in 1855, and as nearly as may be one-half less than they were in 1852, as will be presently seen; and more than half less than those of Harvard University.

The classical studies for pass-men in the Toronto University in 1852 were as follows:

First year.—Homer, Iliad, Bb. VII. and VIII.; Lucian vit.

act. Piscator and Prometheus; Euripides, Medea; Virgil, Æneid, Bb. III. and V.; Horace, Odes, Epodes et Cam. Sæculare, satires Bb. I. and II., Epis.., B. II.

Second year.—Æschines, adv. Ctesiphontem; Sophocles, Œ lipus Rex; Cicero, pro Milone, Phil. II; Juvenal, Sat. III., X., XIII., and XIV.; besides, in the department of ethics, Cicero de Officiis and de Amicitia—not embraced in the present course.

According to the Toronto University College Calendar for 1859-60, the *pass* classical studies for the first two years are as follows:

"*First year.*—Homer, Iliad; B. I, Lucian, Charon and Vita; Virgil, Æneid, B. VI.; Cicero de Amicitia; Translation into Latin prose."

"*Second year.*—Homer, Odessey, B. XI; Demosthenes, Olynthiacs; Horace, Odes; Cicero, Orat. In Catalinam, pro Archia, pro Marcello; Translation into Latin prose." No translations into *Greek* in either of these years; nor in either of the two subsequent years.

It is thus seen how meagre is the required classical course for the undergraduates of the first and second years in University College in comparison of what it was in 1852; and at the end of these two years the student may end his classical studies in the College if he pleases, and yet become B. A., and in due time A. M. In *Victoria College* the classical course of the first two years exceeds that of the University, so does that of the second two years; and no student can there take his degree without having passed the classical course prescribed *during the whole four years.* In Trinity College also there is *no option whatever* in the pass course from matriculation to taking the degree of B. A.

Let us now look at the first two years *classical* studies required of every student at the Harvard University. We have seen that the standard of matriculation is a full year's work higher at Harvard than at Toronto. Now look at the first two years *classical* work in that University. It is as follows:

FIRST YEAR, *Greek.*—The Prometheus of Æschylus; Homer's Odessey, three books; The Panegaricus of Isocrates; Felton's Greek Historians [Thucydides]; Lysias; Greek Antiquities; Exercises in writing Greek.—*Latin.*—Livy [Lincoln's selections]; Horace, Odes and Epodes; Cicero de Senectute and de Amicitia; Zumpt's Grammar; Ramsay's Elementary Manual of Roman Antiquities; Exercises in writing Latin.

SECOND YEAR, *Greek*—Demosthenes, both terms; Grote's History of Greece, vol. xi.; Exercises in writing Greek.—*Latin,*

Cicero pro Sestio; Satires and Epistles of Horace, Beck's Syntax and Zumpt's Grammar; Exercises in writing Latin.

Such is the first two year's course of classical studies required of every student in Harvard, with a still more comprehensive one for the third year, including Modern Greek once a week, and Latin Exercises and Extemporalia. And in Harvard there is no option for any student in classics until the *fourth* year. An option is allowed in *Mathematics* during the third year; but no option in classics until during the fourth year. All that is permitted as to optional or "elective studies," is expressed in the following words:

"*All* the studies of the Freshman and Sophomore [first and second] years are *required*, except that French when taken by the Sophomores is taken as an *extra*. In the Junior [third] year, Mathematics, Chemistry, German, French and Spanish are elective studies, and in the Senior [fourth] year, Latin, Greek, and Italian are added to these electives; *all the rest are required*. In the last two years of the College course, each student must take one of the elective studies assigned to his class; he is also allowed to take another as an *extra*. The elective study when chosen, becomes a required study for that year to those who choose it, and credit is given for it in the scale of rank, as in the case of required studies; but no credit is given for *extra* studies."

It is thus seen that two years *must* be devoted by every student to Mathematics, and three years to Classics.

In *Yale* College there are three terms each year; and there options in classics are permitted only two terms during the four years, in order to take the higher Mathematics. The regulations are as follows:

"Those students who are desirous of pursuing the higher branches of Mathematics are allowed to choose Analytical Geometry in place of the regular Mathematics in the third term of the Sophomore [second] year, and the differential and Integral Calculus, during the first two terms of the Junior [third] year, in place of the Greek and Latin studies of those terms. During the third term of the Junior year, *in addition* to the required studies of the term, the members of the class receive at their option instruction in the French and German Languages, in select Greek or Latin, or in Mineralogy."

All that we have said in respect to the course of classical studies applies equally to the course of Mathematical studies in Toronto, Yale, and Harvard Colleges. It is perfectly clear, therefore, that the prescribed course of studies is much more symmetrical, solid, and complete in the latter than in the former. It is known that Classical and Mathematical studies are pursued much further in the

English than in the American Universities; and, therefore, a comparison with the latter would exhibit in a still stronger light the distorted and pompous littleness of the Toronto system. The various natural science and kindred optional studies with which the Toronto University College course is crammed, are special studies, any one of which a young man can pursue to a much greater extent in the same time, and to a much better purpose when occasion requires, than he can during his college course, where his whole time and strength should be concentrated on what all men of science and literature have agreed as to the studies essential to mental discipline and sound scholarship; and it is only the minor, and what have been called the "one horse colleges" in the neighbouring States that profess to teach every thing, and where every student, young or old, can select at pleasure from a table of options almost as bountiful as that spread by the University College of Toronto, and having performed his optional work, departs in due time with a degree of B.A., though he would have to come to Toronto to get Honors and a Scholarship superadded. But the solid men of New England and of Old England know the worthlessness and injury to sound learning of such an omnibus system; that whatever may be its pretension and show, and however it it may meet the exigencies of many clerical students in the "pursuit of knowledge under difficulties," it is not the method of laying the firm foundation of true science and literature in a country—not the method of raising up a race cultivated, energetic, strong-minded large-hearted men, adapted to their country and their age—not the method of erecting a defined and elevated standard of Liberal Education worthy of a National institution, such as to place the intellect, the science, the literature of Canada upon an honourable, if not equal, footing with that of the most advanced countries of Europe or America.

We have seen how unenviable is our position in regard to the commencement and course of our University College curriculum; and there are still three other points of comparison which we must notice between Toronto and Harvard Colleges before we leave this part of the subject: *First*, the comparative length of the academic year; *secondly*, the number of hours weekly, devoted to instruction; *thirdly*, the number of lectures, or amount of professorial or tutorial assistance given to undergraduates in the pursuit of their studies.

In *Harvard*, the terms and vacations for 1859-60 are as follows: The First Term begins September 1st, and ends January the 18th, with a recess of half a week in November. Then a winter vacation of six weeks. The Second Term begins March 1st, and (with a recess of half a week from the evening

of the 29th of May to the Sunday evening of the 3rd of June,) ends the 18th of July. Then a summer vacation of six weeks.

The vacations and holidays, therefore, amount to just *thirteen weeks*; and the working or academic year to *thirty-nine weeks*. In *Yale*, the vacation and holidays amount to *twelve weeks*, and the academic or working year to *forty weeks*.

In *University College of Toronto*, "the academic year consists of two Terms; the first [Michaelmas], extending from October 1st to December 22nd ; and the second [Easter], from January 7th to May 18th." Vacations from the 22nd of December to the 7th of January, and from the 18th of May to 1st of October—*twenty-one weeks and a half*, besides several holidays during the terms. The vacations and holidays in Toronto University College amount to *twenty-two* weeks—nine weeks more than those of *Harvard*, and ten weeks more than those of *Yale*; and the academic or working year to *thirty weeks*—nine weeks less than those of *Harvard*, and *ten weeks* less than that of *Yale*. Besides, we notice in the calendar, that the *Lectures* in *University College* end the 4th of April—six weeks before the end of the term. If that be for terminal and University examinations, more weeks are devoted to them than days are in *Harvard* and *Yale*.

Next we note the *number of hours each week* devoted to Lectures in *Toronto* and *Harvard* Colleges. [We have not the programme of of Lectures in Yale.] In *Toronto*, the Lectures occupy five days in the week, from four to six hours each day on all subjects, French, German, &c. In *Harvard*, seven hours are devoted each of five days in the week, [from 8 to 1, from 4 to 6,] and two hours on Saturday to Classics, Mathematics, and Ethics, making at least *twelve* hours more lecture work each week at Harvard than at Toronto College. Morning prayers at Harvard are at a quarter before eight one-half of the year, and a quarter before seven the other half of the year; and Lectures in *Classics* and *Mathematics* there invariably begin one-half of the academic year at *nine*, and the other half of the year at *eight* in the morning. In Toronto they never begin before ten. At Harvard habits of early rising and industry are cultivated, which influence the graduates through life.

Lastly, the number of lectures or the amount of professional or tutorial assistance given to the undergraduates in their studies at Toronto and Harvard Colleges presents a contrast still more painful. In Toronto College, the undergraduates are divided into two classes—pass-men and honor-men. In the *first* year, three hours are given each week in Classics to the pass-men, and two hours to the honor-men; it is the same in

Mathematics. In the *second* year, two hours are given weekly in Classics to the pass-men, and two to the honor-men; in Mathematics, one hour per week to pass-men, and three hours to honor-men. In the *fourth* year, two hours per week in both Classics and Mathematics are given to pass-men, and two hours to honor men. The same proportion obtains in the lectures to pass-men and honor-men in other branches. Thus in Toronto College, the pass-men or ordinary undergraduates receive one half less time and assistance from the professors on account of he honor-men, who also are exempted from much pass-work, and have one-half the time of the professors, to enable them to obtain £30 scholarships. In Oxford, the candidates for mathematical honors are not exempt from the pass-work examinations in classics; and *vice versa*. It is so in Harvard and Yale; it is so in both the matriculation and final examinations of the London University. In the English and American colleges the candidates for honors provide their own tutors, as they need, in the prosecution of their honor work. But in Toronto all this is done at the expense of the pass-men. The Toronto system is essentially unjust, partial, and selfish, mars the harmony and symmetry of a collegiate course, and tends to build up one set of men at the expense and to the injury of others. Were it not for this system, each undergraduate would receive twice the time, and therefore twice the amount of assistance in his studies from his professor that he does now. In Harvard College, in the first year, each undergraduate, whether aspiring to honors or not, has six lectures in Latin and six in Greek each week; and four hours in Mathematics. There is the same proportion in subsequent years; and similar differences between the amount of instruction given to each undergraduate in Harvard and Toronto Colleges in other branches.

While, therefore, the academic year in Harvard College is one-fourth longer than it is in Toronto College, and the time given to lectures each week two-sevenths more, the time and assistance given by Professors to each undergraduate is at least twice as much there as here. Four years at Harvard are therefore equal at least to six years at Toronto College. Such a difference need not, ought not to exist. They are both State Colleges; and our State should see that we have not a system established and perpetuated in which there is a maximum of salaries and expenditures with a minimum of labours and benefits, in which there is an elective cosmogony of options, exemptions, teachings, honorships, and scholarships, instead of a system, solid, symmetrical, and practical, just, efficient, and economical, worthy of our country and adapted to exalt its destinies.

We need say but a few words on the last topic under this head—namely, the system of appointing Examiners and conducting the Examinations in the Toronto University. The Examiners selected by an Institution which the Act creating it declared should be separate from any other, and should be national, should, like the judges of the land, be impartial—should be without "fear, favour, or affection" in regard to any school or party: otherwise the selection and proceedings of University Examiners are an expensive farce. A master will, of course, praise his own pupils and magnify his own doings. No one would think of appointing the master of a school as Examiner in order to ascertain its condition and efficiency. This is as true of a College as it is of a school. The words of the Oxford University Regulation are—" *No person can examine a Candidate of the same College or Hall with himself.*" This is a settled principle in the English Universities. In many American Colleges, as also in Victoria College, the authorities select and invite, as far as possible or practical, competent gentlemen wholly unconnected with the College, to act as Committees of Examiners, and report accordingly. In *Harvard* College the Professors have nothing to do with the Examinations. The Governor and Lieutenant Governor of the State, the President of the Senate, and Speaker of the House of Representatives, and thirty other distinguished persons appointed by the Legislature, are a Board of Overseers; and they appoint a Committee " for visiting the University," another Committee " on the Library," another Committee " on the Treasurer's Accounts." There the whole state of the University, and the manner in which it is conducted, and every officer of it performs his duties, and in which all the expenditures are made is carefully examined into. The Overseers also appoint special Committees to conduct all the College Examinations; one Committee "for examination in the Greek Language;" another "for examination in the Latin Language;" a third, in Modern Languages; a fourth, in Rhetoric, Logic, and Grammar; a fifth in Mathematics; a sixth, in Intellectual and Moral Philosophy; a seventh, in Physics; an eighth, in History; a ninth, in Political Economy and Constitutional Law; a tenth, in Chemistry; an eleventh, in Natural History; a twelfth, for visiting the Observatory, &c. Each of these Committees is composed of from twelve to twenty gentlemen, most distinguished for their knowledge of the subject on which they are appointed. They are not paid, as a public spirit and love of country are cultivated among the educated men in the New England States, and they all feel that they owe something to their country for the education they have received. They meet, select certain of their own number to prepare examination papers and conduct the examinations. The College Calendar says,—" Each class is examined

annually, and in writing, in the several studies of the year, before Committees appointed by the Overseers, and the results of these examinations have an important bearing upon the rank of the student, and, in some cases, on his continuance in the College."

How the reverse of all this are the proceedings and examinations in the University and College at Toronto! A report of expenditures is prepared once a year, and audited by a salaried officer of the institution! In the College, the Professor is in every instance either the sole, or first, and of course the principal of two examiners of his own classes, in every department of the College! Take as an example the Classical Department. Never since the establishment of the College has an examination of students in classics been conducted, except by the Classical Professor alone, or by him assisted by one of his own pupils,—his own shadow. In no instance, we believe, has a graduate of another College—much less an Oxford or even Cambridge classic—been selected as Classical Examiner in Toronto University College. The sole authority for the classical attainments of all the students who have ever graduated at Toronto University College, are the commendations of their own Professor; and there are not wanting English critics who allege that their examination are not equal to those of the sixth form of an English Grammar School, and that the classical scholarship thus generated is likely to be kindred to the soda water eloquence by which it is sometimes magnified—effervescent and foaming, with little solidity of substance. But however that be, the system of examinations, like the optional and partial courses of study in the College, would not be tolerated in either Old England or New England.

Is this then the system to be established in Upper Canada, on which alone State endowments, scholarships, and patronage are to be bestowed? And is this the result of all the legislation, expenditures, deliberations and proceedings for the establishment of a Canadian National University? We trust Providence has in store for our country some better fortune than the infliction of such a system upon it. But whatever may be thought of the general question, we think there can be but one opinion as to the necessity of thorough investigation and reform of the system as it now exists —such as has been prayed for by the Wesleyan Conference.

Having thus justified the complaints made by the Wesleyan Conference, we shall in our next and concluding paper, assign several reasons for the liberal system which the Conference advocates in preference to the illiberal, unjust, wasteful, and inefficient system against which we protest— as contrary to the intentions and provisions of the law, condemned by the best examples in England and America, and opposed to the best interests of Upper Canada,

PROOFS AND ILLUSTRATIONS, NO. 8.

Eight facts proved—Policy of monopolists—Eight reasons for the Methodist view of this question—It is the most LIBERAL—most JUST—best adapted to develop voluntary effort—most economical—most promotive of individual and wide-spread interest in behalf of academical education—provides the greatest facilities for its attainment—(testimony of the present President of University College on this point)—tends to elevate the standard of liberal education—most favorable to the moral and religious interests of students—objections answered—first, that the Methodist view is SECTARIAN—(the inconsistency and absurdity of this objection exposed)—second objection, that it endows Roman Catholic Seminaries—answered and retorted—third objection as to the multiplication of colleges—answered by examples and arguments furnished by the present President of University College—the two systems submitted—claims of Victoria College—reasons for undertaking this discussion—conclusion.

In this paper we conclude, for the present, the discussion of the University and College questions. In the preceding seven papers we have not attempted the full discussion of these questions, but have so far discussed the facts connected with them as to justify the Complaints of the Wesleyan Conference and its prayer for Parliamentary inquiry and action. Among other things we think we have clearly proved the following facts:

1. That by passing the University Act in 1853, the Legislature intended to establish a Provincial University as a deliberative and examining body, exclusively, like the London University.

2. That the Legislature recognized and approved the establishment of Colleges in different parts of Upper Canada, and that youth should be encouraged to pursue their studies in them.

3. That the University endowment, after providing what was necessary for the current expenses of the University and College at Toronto and necessary repairs and improvements to the buildings, was to form a distinct Fund to be applied under the direction of Parliament for the promotion of academical education generally in the country.

4. That the erection of new and expensive buildings, and the exclusive building up of one college at Toronto, is entirely contrary to the declared objects and whole scope of the University Act.

5. That the expenditures in regard to both Upper Canada and University Colleges, as well as the University, are large and lavish beyond all precedent, even during the former years of complaint respecting such expenditures.

6. That the Senate of the University, by its composition and proceedings, is divested of all character of nationality, and can only be viewed, as it has only acted, as the exclusive patron and partizan of one College, and not the impartial representative and guardian of all the liberal educational interests of the whole Province.

7. That the proceedings of the Senate have lowered the standard of liberal education, instead of elevating it, as contemplated by the Legislature in passing the University Act

8. That the course of studies, with unnumbered variations, in University College, the system of scholarships and examinations, (apart from the reduction of labor on the part of both professors and undergraduates) are at variance with the examples of both the English, and best American Universities.

Now, what difference of opinion there may be as to the question of a Provincial University consisting of only one, or of various colleges, there can be but one opinion as to the above established facts; and in every view the evils thus proved (and all has not been told) should be corrected. But such is the blinding influence of interest and party, that there are men and presses who are ever keen and on the alert to ferret out and expose real or alleged abuses, who are blind and dumb in regard to University and College abuses, which, if they existed in connexion with any public Department, would cause the head of it to be driven from public life. Advocates of free trade in everything else, are not only protectionists, but advocates of monopoly in Liberal Education? Professed champions of free discussion on all public questions, view, like the promoters of despotism in Italy, free discussion as a great evil in regard to collegiate monopoly, by which they and their friends profit.

We have now to offer some reasons for the University and College system advocated by the Wesleyan Conference and to answer some objections to it. Let it then be recollected, first, that the Wesleyan Conference desires a Provincial University, such as is defined and declared to be intended by the University Act; and secondly, that the several colleges which are or may be connected with it should be placed upon equal footing on equal terms in regard to public aid. Our monopolist opponents maintain that public aid should be given to only one College of the University, and be withheld from all others—the reverse of the declared objects of the University Act.

In support of our view of this great question, we submit in brief the following eight reasons:

1. It is the most *liberal*. To all those who desire a non-denominational College at Toronto, we say, retain it as you desire, and let its minimum endowment not only be equal to, but even twice that of any other college such as we or others prefer, though its number of undergraduates may be less. But while we agree to the State-endowment of your non-denominational College, we demand public aid for our denominational College in proportion to the Collegiate (not denominational) work it does—The Collegiate work as prescribed by a national non-denominational *University*. There are many more undergraduates attending the denominational Colleges in Upper Canada than the non-denominational College. Therefore more than half the inhabitants of Upper Canada prefer the former to the latter. Now, we propose to meet the views of both classes of inhabitants, and our opponents insist upon meeting the views of only one class, and that only one class shall be aided according to their views in the work of collegiate education. Who are the liberals, and who are the monopolists on this question?

2. Our view is also most *just*, as well as most liberal. The advocates of denominational colleges are individually subscribers for their erection and support. Clergy and Laity act in common; the one has no advantage or interest different from the other, except that the former perhaps subscribe more largely and generally in proportion to their means than the latter. In all other respects their interests and labours are one. They procure their own college premises and erect their own college buildings, and contribute also to support their College. The advocates of a non-denominational College do nothing of all this. They hang upon the State or public for everything. Their system is one of individual selfishness. They do nothing, they give nothing; they suck the public for everything. Yet they object that any public aid should be given to those who so largely give and help themselves. Which system and which class of persons are the just and which the unjust? The one class says, we do to others as we would others should do to us; the other class says, give us all, and give nothing to others. The one class do more themselves than they ask the public to do; the other class does nothing but say, like the grave, " give, give," without ever having enough.

3. The system we advocate is the best and the only one adapted to *develop voluntary effort*. Ours is an age and a country of voluntary effort; and those systems of social progress are most prosperous and useful that are based upon it. Such is

our Common School system. The people must meet and organize, and provi their own school-house, and employ their teacher, —that is, put forth individually and collectively these voluntary efforts—before they acquire a title or claim to public aid. Why should not those who acquire collegiate education for their sons be required to perform the same conditions as those who can only give their sons a common school education? We advocate the same conditions in both cases; and this our opponents oppose. The establishment and management of higher seminaries of learning being the peculiar province (and requiring the combined efforts) of a religious denomination, as the establishment and management of a common school are the appropriate province and require the collective efforts of a school section, we maintain that the religious community when it erects its collegiate or seminary buildings and engages its Professors, should have its voluntary efforts supplemented and encouraged by public aid, just as the School Section has its voluntary efforts supplemented by an apportionment from the School Fund according and in proportion to its own works. Our opponents say, "No, we will do nothing ourselves for academical education; we demand the State to do everything for us; and we forbid the State doing anything for you, how much soever you may do yourselves." The advocates for public aid to denominational seminaries put their own shoulders to the wheel before they ask help from the State Hercules helping others at all, but cry out for all his strength to be employed in their behalf, though they do not so much as put forth their little finger to help themselves. Who are the true voluntaries, then, and who the sham voluntaries, the real non-voluntaries on this question? And which is the true and only system to develop voluntary effort in behalf of higher, as well as elementary education?

4. Our system is also the *most economical*. The expenditures which have been made in connection with Upper Canada and University Colleges, and of which we have briefly treated in the fifth of these papers, illustrate the economy of the system of our opponents. Had the expenditures for Upper Canada and University Colleges, been made upon the condition that the friends of them should provide a certain proportion of the sums expended, who does not believe that there would have been rigid economy instead of almost incredible lavishness in their expenditures, and that one thousand pounds could have done more than two thousand pounds have done? Economy, as a general rule, is an essential element of voluntaryism in the support of its institutions. Where public appropriation is combined with voluntary effort, and is made dependent upon it, the latter is greatly increased in exertion by the inducements of the former,

and the former is applied with increased economy by the influence of the latter. But institutions like the Upper Canada and University Colleges, from which voluntaryism is altogether excluded, and where every man is interested in getting all the money he can, and pays nothing, will ever be, as they have always been, a bottomless pit of expenditures and expensiveness, with comparatively paltry returns for the outlay. Even the State Colleges of Harvard and Yale largely depend upon their own efforts and success for their support and the salaries of their Professors and Tutors, as do the English and Irish Colleges. But in Toronto everything is done and paid for by the State; the individual gives nothing, receives all; full salaries are paid by the State, and a periodical increase of them. Which then is the most economical, the system which combines voluntary effort with public appropriation, or that which does nothing itself and receives everything from the State? And who are the true economists in a system of academical education, those who ask public aid in proportion to, and as a supplement to their own doings, or those who, prodigal like, receive and spend the state patrimony by tens of thousands, but give not a penny themselves?

5. Our system likewise is most promotive of individual and wide-spread interest in behalf of academical education. Persons think of and value that to which they contribute. Since the people have learned to contribute, and to impose upon themselves contributions to the common schools, they have valued them more, improved them more, and sent more children to them, than they ever did before. In the neighboring State of New York, contributions to establish Seminaries and Colleges are general, and every man there above poverty is most anxious and ambitious to give both his sons and daughters a superior education; and the State developes and encourages this individual and wide-spread interest in higher education by promoting and supplementing its efforts. Hundreds of youths have already been sent to Victoria College, who would have been kept at home in comparative ignorance, but for the interest thus excited in the minds of their parents and friends; nor could the College have been sustained but for the suplementary co-operation of the State. Thus is the voluntary system with all its advantages brought into full play by the conditional and proportional co-operation of the State, and the latter makes up the deficiencies of the former. The doctrine of the Toronto Monopolist advocates, repudiates the voluntary system in Collegiate education, paralyzes individual effort, deadens individual feeling, and substitutes a cold-hearted individual selfishness for warm and active individual sympathy. It is a system of leech-

like hanger-on-ship upon the State, without a single pulsation of individual enterprise and patriotism.

6. And while our system is most promotive of individual interest in academical education, it adds proportionately to *its facilities.* The Legislature in the preamble of the University Act, says that "many parents and others are deterred by the expense and other causes, from sending the youth under their charge to be educated in a large city distant, in many cases, from their homes," and that "from these and other causes, many do and will prosecute and complete their studies in other institutions in various parts of this Province, *to whom it is just and right* to afford facilities for obtaining those scholastic honors and rewards which their dilligence and proficiency may deserve, and thereby to encourage them and others to persevere in the pursuit of knowledge and sound learning." This is the spirit and working of the system which we advocate. It recognizes and promotes the establishment of Seminaries of education in different parts of the Province, and thus increases the facilities of sound learning. In 1845, two years after the introduction of Mr. Baldwin's first Bill to make King's College a Provincial University, and on the printing of Mr. Draper's bill for the same purpose, a well written pamphlet of 67 pages, entitled "The University Question Considered," was printed by Mr. Rowsell, was understood and as evinced by ample internal evidence to have been written by the present President of University College, under the signature of "*A Graduate.*" In this pamphlet the author advocated King's College being retained and restored as a Church of England Institution, and the endowment by Parliament of other Colleges, and eloquently argued against the establishment of a centralized system of University education, and against the establishment of a non-denominational University at Toronto as infidel in principal, godless in character, impracticable in management, expensive in operations, and more than doubtful in results. Speaking of a system which would require all persons to come to Toronto in order to avail themselves of the benefits of University Education, the author says—"There can be no doubt, that there are many parents who would not only complain of this as a heavy tax, but would regard with aversion any plan, whereby their children would be removed from their care, and left without their supervision amidst the temptations of a large town. Nor can it be questioned, that many would thus be wholly excluded, by the narrowness of their circumstances, from affording their sons the advantages of the University—whilst some would prefer foregoing them to running the risk necessary for their enjoyment," (p. 40.)—This is almost the very language of the preamble of

the University Act, as also of the Memorial of the Wesleyan Conference; and we may well therefore say of our system, in the words of the same Pamphlet—"It would distribute through the Province the advantages which a University brings to the place in which it is situated, and to the whole country in its vicinity, instead of securing a monopoly of these to any one district. It would render the blessings of University education more easily and cheaply accessible to a greater number of the community."

7. In the sixth and seventh of these papers, we have shown how the present Toronto system has reduced the standard and injured the symmetry and soundness of University College education. On the contrary in two respects will the system for which we argue, tend to elevate the standard of University education. A University commission or Body not identified with any one College, but equally independent and impartial in regard to all, would be the most likely to establish and maintain a high, sound, and practical standard of University studies and examinations—the examinations and scholarships, like those of the London University, being confined to matriculation and graduation—leaving the Scholarships and examinations of the intervening years (established at Toronto to build up University College) to the several Colleges themselves; and the candidates for University Scholarships and honors not being exempted, as they are not in the London or the English Universities from examination in all the pass subjects, should receive Scholarships and honors only for doing the regular work in the superior manner, or doing extra work in extra subjects. Then, in the next place let candidates come from the several Colleges for matriculation or degrees, before others than their own Tutors—before an impartial committee—and the reputation, and appropriations to such Colleges in part depending on the success of their Students at these Examinations. Who does not see that such a system tends far more to elevate the standard of University education; than the present system, so partial and disjointed in itself, and so un-British and convent-like in the examination of its Students by their own professional Tutors. In several of our best Grammar Schools, there is a strong competition, and boys are prepared in a manner unprecedented and admirable to compete for Matriculation Scholarships and honors. Place Colleges in the same position of equality and competition, in regard to collegiate education, and higher and larger results will enevitably follow. But a Provincial University should also encourage by rewards and distinctions, studies and proficiency in the several branches of Science and the useful arts as well as in the subjects of University Education.

8. Finally, our system is the most favorable to the moral and religious interest of students, and therefore of the country. We believe there is scarcely a parent in Canada who would not far rather send his son to a denominational College not of his own religious persuasion, where that son would be under truly religious care and instruction, than to send such a son to a non-denominational college where "no man cares for his soul," and he is left in the midst of temptation without the shield of parental oversight or the counsels of pastoral instruction, and whence he perhaps returns home after years of absence, with a more cultivated mind, but with a vitiated heart and ruined principles. In the words of the Conference Memorial, "experience shows that, while pastoral and parental care can be exercised for the religious instruction of children residing at home and attending a day school, that care cannot be exercised over youth residing away from home and pursuing their higher education except in a college where the pastoral and parental care can be daily combined. We hold that the highest interests of the country, as of an individual, are its religious and moral interests; and we believe there can be no heavier blow dealt out against those religious and moral interests than for a youth of a country destined to receive the best literary education, to be placed, during the most eventful years of that educational course, without the pale of daily parental and pastoral instruction and oversight. The results of such a system must, sooner or later, sap the religious and moral foundations of society. For such is the tendency of our nature, that with all the appliances of religious instruction and ceaseless care by the parent and pastor, they are not always successful in counteracting evil propensities and temptations; and therefore from a system which involves a withdrawal and absence of all such influences for years at a period when youthful passions are strongest and youthful temptations most powerful, we cannot but entertain painful apprehensions. Many a parent would deem it his duty to leave his son without the advantages of a liberal education, rather than thus expose him to the danger of moral shipwreck in its requirement."

We have now to reply to several objections; and while replying to these, we shall offer additional reasons for denominational colleges, and in behalf of Victoria College in particular.

1. It is objected that our system is "sectarian,"—that is, denominational. This is the staple cry, and almost sole argument against our system. Yet it does merit the name of argument, and involves such glaring absurdities that we have been surprised how any Christian man could employ it without self-condemnation and shame. It implies that denominationalism is a calamity to be lamented, and that denominational instruction is an evil to be de-

precated. Yet our country is filled with this very evil, if evil it be ; and it is promoted by the instruction of more than a thousand ministers, and is voluntarily embraced and supported as a privilege and a blessing by nearly the entire population! If the people themselves are denominational, why should not their colleges be denominational? If denominational instruction is good on Sundays, why is it not good during the week ? If a parent wishes his son to be in intimate connection with his own denomination at home, and under its most careful instructions, why should he not desire the same for him abroad? and that daily, morning and evening, and at all times, with a mother's love, and a father's earnestness, and a chief Shepherd's vigilance and tenderness? The instinctive impulse of parental piety and religious consistency furnishes the best reply to this absurd objection. Even in regard to denominational day schools, no well informed man has ever objected to such schools as evil in themselves. No Episcopalian, or Presbyterian, or Baptist, or Methodist can doubt that a school conducted by a pious and competent teacher of his own church, with its catechisms, devotions, and ministerial instructions, would not be as good a school as any non-denominational school. The objection to denominational day schools is, that the requisite accommodations and teachers cannot be provided for them without an expense impossible to be borne, and that the religious instruction necessary for all children in a day school, can be provided for otherwise than in the school, *as the children are with their parents mornings and evenings, and Sabbaths*, and that a school cannot be provided for all the children in each neighborhood without the combination of all classes of the inhabitants. But while a denominational day school is the most economical and effectual means of providing for the common school education of all the children of a neighbourhood, we have shown that the denominational colleges are the most economical and effectual means of providing superior education for all the youth of the country,— as well as for their best moral and religious interests. The religious denominations constitute the Christianity of the country, and its best interests depend upon the fidelity and care with which the ministers and parents of the different denominations religiously instruct their own youth. Must not those colleges, then, be most desirable in which the duties and influences of the parent and the pastor can be combined in the highest degree in behalf of youth during several of the most critical and eventful years of their life, when they are absent from home, and during their most important courses of educational instruction ? Are the English and Scotch University graduates now resident in Canada the worst men for having been educated in denominational colleges? Are they monsters to be avoided until they abandon the faith of

5

their collegiate education? Do they believe it better to be educated with no religious principles and feelings than with decided religious principles and feelings? Do they regard as a calamity what is the glory of England and Scotland? We appeal to every Presbyterian minister in Canada who has been educated in Scotland, whether he regards the religious influences of his collegiate education as an evil and not a benefit, and whether he does not believe it would have been better rather than worse for him had those religious influences been more powerful, more constant, more practical than they were?

Nothing, therefore, is more unreasonable and absurd than the cry against "sectarian" Colleges. It *cannot* be the dictate of denominational *principle*; for if so, its authors would be bound in consistency to abandon their denominationalism altogether. It may be the tactics of the monopolist to retain his unjust gains; or it may be the policy of the enemy of religious instruction in any form; or it may be the cry of denominational jealousy and bigotry, lest others should receive more than ourselves, instead of the manly, just, and honourable feeling that if my neighbour does more than I do, he ought to receive more than I receive.

But it is also to be borne in mind that no aid is asked or received to support or teach sectarianism, but for supporting those who, though they hold and act upon the doctrines of some sect, are teaching languages, mathematics, philosophy, &c., in which there is neither religious nor political sectarianism; nor then until after the religious persuasion whose College is thus aided in supporting its Professors, has largely contributed to the same object, and assumes all the responsibility and labour of carrying it into effect. If any advantage accrues to the agency in this work, it is indirect and remote, and is what is experienced by any city, town, or body in whose vicinity a public institution may be situated. The real question for the consideration of the statesman and philanthropist is, in what way can each pound of the University endowment be made instrumental in educating the largest number of youth in the higher branches, with the best preventions against impairing or endangering their morals? This is the great object to be considered; and if in promoting this object in the most efficient and economical manner for the general welfare, some advantage should accrue to the agencies employed, it remains for the objector to show that such incidental advantage, for so great a public benefit and so much labour, would be unjust in itself, or a calamity to be dreaded.

2. It is also objected that the system we advocate endows Roman Catholic Seminaries. The objectors who urge this objection omit two things. They omit to say that the principle they

advocate involves the equity, and no doubt in a short time the necessity of employing Roman Catholic Professors, as well as Protestant, in their College, which is avowedly founded upon the principle of equal justice to all parties. Have not the Roman Catholics as good a right to a representation in the professorships and teachings of the University College as the Protestants ? And will they not claim it ? And can they be refused it ? The objectors likewise omit to say that under the present system—and notwithstanding all that certain parties have said or pretended to say, it has increased the last ten years, and will doubtless continue to increase—the Roman Catholics have already grants to three Colleges in Upper Canada. Now we ask the objectors themselves whether it is not better to place such institutions upon the same footing with others—upon the ground of *work*—and not upon that of Church interference; and of work, too, in subjects common to both Protestants and Roman Catholics ? And can they deny that the Roman Catholic is a man and a British subject, and has rights as such as well as themselves, whatever may be his errors ? We cannot omit adding, how oddly this objection comes from those who are known to have courted alliance with that very section of the Roman Catholics who are the most ultra and exacting in regard to education as well as public offices.

3. The only other objection requiring notice is, that the system we advocate encourages the multiplication of Colleges, and that these Colleges will be small and attended by few Students. In reply, we remark that as the building for each College or Seminary is erected by the parties establishing it, and not by the Government, they best know their own wants and means, that though the number of such Institutions may make a difference in the amount of public aid apportioned to each—like the number of schools in a municipality—it can make no difference in the aggregate endowment or grant for Academical Education. In favour of a number of Colleges and of even University Colleges, instead of one, the eloquent author of the pamphlet of 1845, above quoted, adduces numerous examples. He shows that in Prussia there are six Universities ; in Austria, ten; in the Kingdom of Sardinia, four; in Belgium, four ; in Holland, three ; and significantly adds: "France, indeed, furnishes a precedent for having but one University, but it must be remembered that the principle of " the Royal University" in that kingdom is not *centralization* but *dispersion*, for there are about twenty-six Colleges under it, scattered over the country."—(p. 60.) Then, in answer to the argument for consolidation from the example of the London University, the author of the pamphlet says, "its characteristic is *dispersion not centralization*, for it recognizes for degrees in Arts and Law the certificates of not less than twenty-one (now thirty-eight) Col-

leges or institutions scattered over England, Wales, and Ireland; whilst those who receive degrees in Medicine, embrace students of more than sixty establishments in different parts of the world."— (page 49.) In connection with the Universities of Oxford and Cambridge, there are upwards of forty Colleges. The authority of example and the testimony of experience are, therefore, in favour of a number of Colleges and against centralization in one.

Then as to the number of students in a college, that cannot affect its efficiency, unless they are too numerous. Large classes in either a School or Colleges are a disadvantage rather than an advantage to the pupils themselves. On this point the author of the University pamphlet quoted above (and who writes from experience) justly remarks that "the Professors must for some years be content to discharge chiefly the duties of tutors; and under these circumstances, the smallness of their classes is rather an advantage inasmuch as it enables them fully to test the preparation and ascertain the deficiencies of each of the Students on every occasion of attendance."—(p. 61,62). There are wealthy Colleges at Oxford that will not receive over fifty Students; and there are Colleges both in England and Ireland in which there are not half that number. But no party would incur the expense and responsibility of establishing a College or Seminary without a moral certainty of a sufficient number of Students to employ the strength of any tutor or professor. Then,

Lastly, as to the number of professors required in a College, the author of the pamphlet is good authority and remarks as follows: "The other Universities, [besides that of King's College] should be endowed so as to enable them to have sufficient schools of Arts and divinity, and also to have good preparatory Seminaries attached to them. *The Head, with four Professors would be fully equal, for some years, to the discharge of the University duties.* This, indeed, is a stronger staff than King's College [now University College] at present possesses in those faculties."—[p. 56.] Of course a divinity school or divinity professors form no part of our plan. As the parties establishing Colleges, provide the buildings, &c., themselves, the public aid can and ought only to apply to the salaries of the four or five professors. That such a number is ample in the faculty of Arts is not only clear from the example and authority adduced, but from the fact that in a College with a four years' course, there are but four classes of Students, each Professor could meet even daily each of his four classes. With one Professor in each of the four branches of a collegiate course, each class of undergraduates could be provided with a daily lecture, if need be, in each subject of their studies; and we submit to any disinterested man of common sense, whether if, estimating the University income endow-

ment at £15,000 per annum [much below what has been reported] the payment of £1,500 a year to each of ten staffs of Professors in ten Colleges in different parts of the province, and the Students from all those Colleges coming up for matriculation and degree examinations to one central body, would not do vastly more to promote liberal education in Upper Canada, than to spend the whole £15,000 a-year on one College in Toronto with one staff of professors?

But, on the other hand, suppose instead of a Provincial University, the system of various University Colleges be preferred,—as the present President of Toronto University College formerly contended—we ask, are not the other University Colleges in Upper Canada entitled to public aid as well as University College at Toronto? We leave those connected with other colleges to speak for themselves; but in respect to *Victoria College* we may say, that it was the first academy of learning erected in Upper Canada by voluntary effort; that its doors have ever been open to the pupils of all religious denominations with most scrupulous care of their morals and their rights as desired by their parents; that since 1834, it has educated some thousands of youth of various religious denominations, who are now engaged in almost every profession and employment in the country; that its students, with very few exceptions, like its teachings, have been characterized by sound knowledge, good sense, energy of character, love of country and religion, and an ardent zeal and effort to promote education and benevolent institutions; that it contains an admirable preparatory school for the elementary English and classical education of children; that it provides special courses of instruction for that considerable class of meritorious youth, and young men who cannot aspire to a University education, but who aim at more than a common school education, and require instruction in special branches for special employments; that it has prepared a very large number of this class of young men for respectable and useful pursuits in life; that it provides a thorough course of collegiate education, second to none in Upper Canada, evincive of which two of its students have been admitted *ad eundem* from its third year's course into the fourth year's course of the Toronto University College, proceeded to and took their degree of B. A. in the University of Toronto the same month they would have taken it had they remained in the University of Victoria College, and also a medical gentleman who received the whole of his literary education at Victoria College, and the whole of his medical education in the school of the Dean of the Medical Faculty of Victoria College, has been twice selected by the Toronto University over all the other Medical gentlemen in Upper Canada, as sole Examiner for the University in Anatomy

and Physiology; that Victoria College has, according to the Catalogue of '59, 60 students in the Faculty of Arts, 73 students in the Faculty of Medicine, and 155 special students and pupils in the preparatory Grammar and English School. In every relation therefore, whether as a University College, or the college of a University, and in every aspect, whether for the number of its pupils or students, the efficiency of its preparatory school, or the thoroughness and practical character of its collegiate instructions, whether from the elevation of its moral character and influence, or the length and value of its services, it has the strongest claim upon the liberality of the Legislature as it has upon the gratitude and confidence of the country. The denial of its just claims, and the proscriptions of them as well as of kindred rights, by the perversion of the University Act, and the misapplication of the country's noblest liberality in the University endowment, has imposed upon us the painful task of the present investigations. As the party most wronged and injured, we have been the first to complain of our wrongs, and to vindicate our rights, and in doing so to assert and maintain the rights of others. We now submit whether we have not had ample grounds for making our complaints, and whether we have presented ample reasons for asserting our rights—right against monopoly and proscription, rights of equal regard to the views and wishes of one half of the community with the other half in matters pertaining to the education and welfare of their offspring. We also submit whether we have not, in maintaining what is dear to ourselves as parents, as Christians, and as citizens, we have but maintained that which must accord with the views and interests of the greatest number of our fellow subjects, which is calculated to correct evils and promote economy in the expenditure of the most sacred of our public funds, which will provide the best education for the largest number of Canadian youth upon the truest Christian principles, and open up a future to our country, for which posterity may remember us with respect and gratitude!

CONTENTS.

INTRODUCTION.
Appeal of the Wesleyan Conference in favour of the Diffusion of Liberal Education throughout Upper Canada..................

MEMORIAL.
The Memorial prepared by order and on behalf of the Conference of the Wesleyan Methodist Church in Canada....................

PROOF AND ILLUSTRATION OF THE STATEMENTS IN THE CONFERENCE MEMORIAL, No. 1.
The Monopolists' fallacy exposed—Difference between a University and College—Examples—Prizes and Scholarships by wholesale—Views of the Wesleyan Body on the Question of a Provincial University, including the Colleges of the country, since 1843... 11

PROOF AND ILLUSTRATION OF THE MEMORIAL, No. 2.
First complaint of the Wesleyan Conference justified—The objects of the University Act, as declared in the Preamble and 3rd Section, defeated by the past proceedings and present composition of the Senate... 16

PROOFS AND ILLUSTRATIONS, No. 3.
Question stated.—Clauses of the Act authorizing expenditures of University Funds quoted—"Current Expenses" and "additions and improvements" to existing buildings alone authorized—Wherein the provisions of the Act have been perverted and violated in the expenditures of moneys, and in the application of the SURPLUS Income Fund for 1856—Increased Expenses of University College since 1845 and 1853—Evils of FUSING together the management of the University and University College—Violation of an important principle of political economy and good government. Memorial for Parliamentary investigation and interference justified............ 20

PROOFS AND ILLUSTRATIONS, No. 4.
Recapitulation—Misquotations and misrepresentations of the *Christian Messenger* and Montreal *Witness* adduced and exposed—Methodist plan of a Provincial University and Superior Education—The *Leader's* argumentation—Three reasons why the Wesleyan Conference has originated the present appeal to the country and to the Legislature..................... 26

PROOFS AND ILLUSTRATIONS, No. 5.
Expenditures connected with Upper Canada College, the University, University College and Scholarships—Contrast between the London and Toronto Universities as to expenditures, Buildings, and Scholarships—Extravagance, injustice and folly of the Toronto University, Grammar School, College and Scholarship Systems exposed.............................. 34

PROOFS AND ILLUSTRATIONS, No. 6.

Objects of a Provincial University—Threefold Argument against the Toronto System stated—A four fold answer to an objection—Present Standard of admission to University College shown to be much lower than that of 1852, before the passing of the University Act, and a full year's work lower than that of Harvard College, near Boston, while the *work* during the four years' course of study is an Academical year less than that of Harvard College—Teaching of Grammar School, Theological Students in Toronto, a reason for reducing the University College course of instruction.......................... 40

PROOFS AND ILLUSTRATIONS, No. 7.

Objects of Collegiate Studies—Options and Exemptions during three out of the four years of the present University College Course—their baneful tendency and effects—the classical pass-work, or required undergraduate classical studies of the first two years in Toronto University College in 1852 and 1859-60, and in Harvard College, compared—the Toronto classical first two years' course one half now what it was in 1852, and less than half that of Harvard and Yale Colleges compared with those of Toronto University College—effects of them contrasted—Academic year nine weeks longer, twelve hours more work per week, and more than twice the amount of professional instruction and assistance given to undergraduates at Harvard than at Toronto—Injustice of the Toronto system of college lectures to pass undergraduates, compared with the English and Harvard systems—Toronto University system of appointing Examiners and conducting Examinations of students the reverse of the University examination system of Old England and New England—Contrasts and Conclusion... 46

PROOFS AND ILLUSTRATIONS, No. 8.

Eight facts proved—Policy of monopolists—Eight reasons for the Methodist view of this question—It is the most LIBERAL—most JUST—best adapted to develop voluntary effort—most economical—most promotive of individual and wide-spread interest in behalf of academical education—provides the greatest facilities for its attainment—(testimony of the present President of University College on this point)—tends to elevate the standard of liberal education—most favorable to the moral and religious interests of students—objections answered—first, that the Methodist view is SECTARIAN—(the inconsistency and absurdity of this objection exposed)—second objection, that it endows Roman Catholic Seminaries—answered and retorted—third objection as to the multiplication of colleges—answered by examples and arguments furnished by the present President of University College—the two systems submitted—claims of Victoria College—reasons for undertaking this discussion—conclusion.......... 57

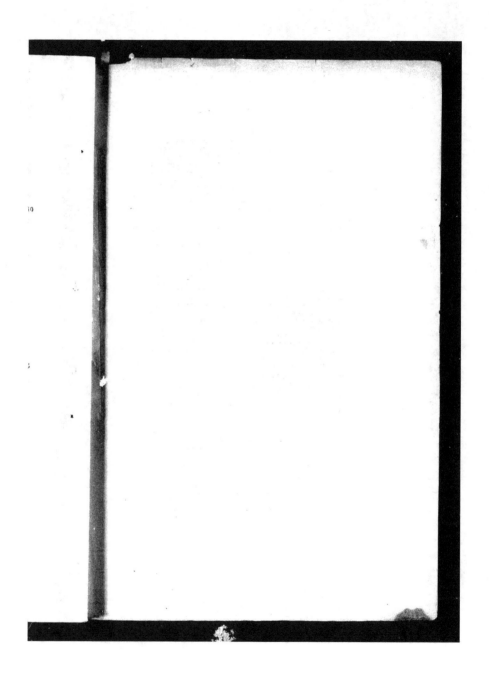

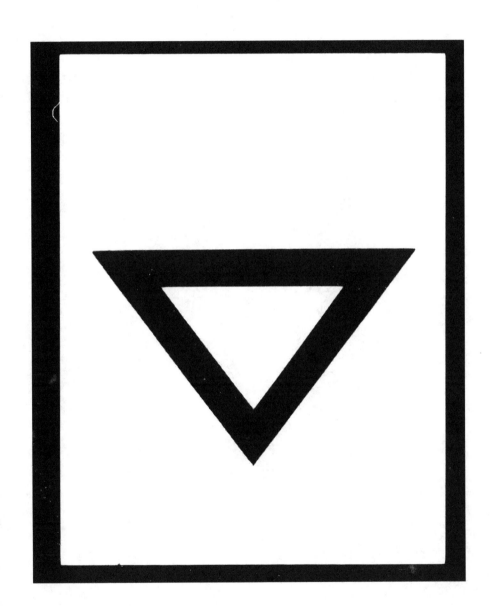